WHAT IT WAS:

GROWING UP
WHEN THE MUSIC MATTERED

BY JAMES PAGLIASOTTI

New Northwest Productions

Center for the
New Northwest

WHAT IT WAS:

Growing Up When the Music Mattered

by James Pagliasotti

Softcover: ISBN 978-1-7369129-1-1

Printed in the U.S.A.

First edition

You and Bill Wyman, Denver, Colorado 1972

What It Was:

A MOMENT IN TIME when you and a whole lot of other people had the great good fortune to come of age. We gathered to celebrate, dance, drink, dream our dreams and listen to the soundtrack of our lives as we lived them to the fullest.

It was dense with creativity and freedom, care of your sisters and brothers, aspirations for peace and love, a brief but glorious respite between stifling conventionalism and the coming dominance of big commerce, a time the likes of which we may never see again.

I grew up in Colorado, but it doesn't really matter where you were raised: if you came of age in the years after WWII, you grew up when the music mattered. This is what I remember about the 28 year period period from 1951 and 1979—a full Saturn Return cycle unlike any other.

Dedication

TO EVERYONE MENTIONED HEREIN, my thanks. To a greater or lesser degree, you taught me a lot. It was a privilege, a pleasure, and for the most part a rocking good time sharing this life and time with you.

Special thanks to: David A. Casey, Jami Cassady and the Neal Cassady Estate, Stephen Collector, Carole Florian, Megan Friedel, David Givens, Fred Gowdy, Wendy Hall, Richard Kreck, Brian Kreizenbeck, Roy Laird, Heidi Lindy, Chuck Morris, my beautiful sister JoAnne Pagliasotti, Bob Pennetta, Sandy Phelps, David Shepardson, Dianne Stromberg, Craig Swank, Thom Trunnell, Harry Tuft, and Chuck E. Weiss.

To Kate, Sarah, Deva, Dante, and to their families, past, present, future. And especially to Lucretia Weems. Maybe not much but it's what it was. This is for you.

An important note of thanks to Dan Fong, with whom I've collaborated on one project or another in one way or another for many years. Not only did he provide many of the best photographs in this book, he also gave me some advice many years ago about making efforts like this one. He said, "the official history is so corrupt, if you don't take the time to record what it was like to be you in this time we're living, no one in the future will ever know the truth."

'Nuff said.

James Pagliasotti

May 2019

Contents

1

WHAT?

YOU BEGIN IN A LITTLE ROOM IN A LITTLE HOUSE in a little neighborhood. You get to know your neighbors a few at a time. They are Sparr, Mruz, Vannis, Hawkins. Up the street, the Allisons. Over on Krameria, there's even a kid from New York named Jerry Cohen. He knows about the Brooklyn Dodgers and people say he's a Jew. Turns out the Sparrs are Jews, too. The DePriests are called Negroes, so are the Wagners. People say your uncle Freddie Bacca is a Mexican. Little Ernie and Puddy across the alley are shorter than you are and you're only six. They are called midgets. You don't know what all that matters, but it means different. Your family is Catholic, which might be strange, too. There's a lot to learn.

The neighborhood gets a little bigger and you start to get around. There are kids everywhere, lots of them. Someday they'll be called Baby Boomers, but now they're just people you want to know. They live in little houses bought with the G.I. Bill by working class people after the big war. The dads go to work, the moms stay home, the kids have a ball.

Every Sunday, you went to your grandparents' home on 5th and Meade for dinner. They had a television, little green screen in a great big console, but there were no programs. You'd turn it on and stare at the Big Chief test pattern week after week. One day in 1952, the screen changed and on came Gene Autrey all duded up, riding Champion, strumming his guitar, singing "Back in the Saddle Again." It was absolutely astonishing.

Another day, a few years later, you and Doug Allison are in his bedroom listening to the radio and on comes Heartbreak Hotel. Elvis Presley!

Turn it up! Louder! We're playing it full blast and jumping up and down on his bed, screaming at the top of our lungs, pounding on each other with pure joy.

His mother comes in, big busty blond in a slip, hair in curlers, hands over her ears, screaming, "Turn it down, turn it down!" Over and over.

We can't hear her. We can't hear anything but Elvis. Nothing was ever the same again.

Elvis in Full, 1956

Jack Kerouac, Neal Cassady, and friend in 1952; photograph by Carolyn Cassady

2

BEAT

GEOGRAPHY HAD EVERYTHING TO DO WITH IT. Happenstance, too. Denver in those days was a way station, the mid-point for hipsters traveling from New York to San Francisco. Stop in Chicago. Stop in Denver. The Beat Generation was on the road. Denver had Neal Cassady. Visions of Cody. Kerouac's muse.

Local boys Ed White and Hal Chase were the interface between Cassady and the intellectuals at Columbia University, where Kerouac and Allen Ginsberg were among the crowd they palled around with. Cassady to them was a young, hard-driven, picturesque, quasi-criminal product of the Skid Row area of town, a prototypical example of the Beat characters Kerouac described in his rambling portrayal of post-war American life.

Many of those notable Beat figures and their cohorts eventually passed through Denver. Some even stayed a while, including Jack himself (many a time), Ginsberg, Anne Waldman, and William Burroughs, among others. Those latter three in the Seventies would found the Kerouac School of Disembodied Poetics at the Naropa Institute in Boulder, but for now they were just passing through and looking around.

Much of what became the portraiture of Beat literature was based on what Kerouac and his cohorts saw here, and the places they haunted together with Cassady and his friends, many of whom became the iconic characters of their early works. It gave this little cow town a core of recognition among an emerging intellectual, literary, and musical elite.

There were artists, too, like the painter Vance Kirkland and the experimental filmmaker Stan Brakhage, both of whom found critical acclaim in the Sixties and beyond, as the culture in Denver and elsewhere began to open its aperture and see with growing clarity a broader field of what creative people were producing.

Kirkland in the Fifties produced work that made significant contributions to the field of Abstract Expressionism. Brakhage in Denver and San Francisco worked with artists like the poet Kenneth Rexroth and the composer John Cage, among others who came into the cultural community of post-war Colorado, if only tangentially.

Rocking at the Trocadero Ballroom, Elitch Gardens 1950s

Cities around the country were loosely linked by jazz clubs, and the Beats were into that. Experimental art was their thing, too, and pockets of it existed everywhere that freedom of expression was taking hold.

For a town its size, Denver had a strong jazz tradition. Glenn Miller was a native son of Colorado. Big bands like his played the Trocadero Ballroom at Elitch Gardens. His noted clarinetist, Peanuts Hucko, led the World's Greatest Jazz Band with local musicians like pianist Ralph Sutton and many other noted players who regularly joined Dick Gibson's famed jazz parties up in Aspen and later held forth at the Navarre downtown. Max Morath was the local king of Ragtime.

Jazz clubs in Denver were Shaner's and El Chapultepec downtown, the Pic-a-Rib on East Colfax, the Rossonian Hotel, the Turf Club, and the Casino Cabaret in Five Points, clubs where nearly every big name band and singer at one time or another played. There were a few joints like Eddie Bohn's Pig 'n' Whistle, Joe "Awful" Coffee's, and piano bars in various hotels downtown.

Lionel Hampton and friends at the Rossonian Lounge, 1950s

The great Charles Burrell came to town from Michigan to play with the Denver Symphony Orchestra and held court at the Rossonian, where he played with a Hall of Fame list of visiting jazz greats over the years. His niece, Dianne Reeves, and other great players to be like Ron Miles and Bill Frisell grew up in East Denver, where Frisell learned his chops from the celebrated teacher, Dale Brunning. Spike Robinson brought his mellow sax to clubs all over Denver, often with Littleton native, Grammy and Oscar award-winning pianist and composer Dave Grusin. The great guitarist Johnny Smith was a fixture on the scene. That was the jazz nightlife in Denver.

For the adventurous, there was Taylor's Supper Club on West Colfax, which featured a mixed bag of live entertainment, and Warren St. Thomas' Tropics out on Morrison Road, where some of the country's best known ecdysiasts performed. The rich folks went to the Park Lane on Marion Parkway over by Washington Park, the Cosmopolitan on Broadway, or the Brown Palace on Tremont, where in the Ship Tavern Dwight D. Eisenhower one rowdy evening was said to have mooned the room from the Crow's Nest high above the crowd.

Folk music clubs linked cities throughout the country and name acts travelled from Boston and New York to Chicago, Denver, and on to the West Coast, where San Francisco especially was a hot bed of the Beat scene and the music that served it.

The folk music circuit was where the contemporary music business in Denver really began. A fortuitous change in the nature of the business occurred at the intersection of folk music and rock & roll. It put Colorado on the map in a way that brought about the migration of big name musicians to the state.

Unlike pop music, folk music was made of songs that mattered, if only to a select group of people, about serious subjects heard by earnest, thoughtful folks who trended by nature somewhere outside the mainstream. For a time when the Fifties turned into the Sixties, it became a lifestyle unto itself.

Working class protest songs, Wobblies union shouts, Negro blues and spirituals, plaintive country ballads were the stuff of folk music. Social protest over civil rights, the military industrial complex, the burgeoning colossus that corporate business was becoming, the stifling conventionalism of post-war America, all of it coalesced around an alternative way of life with music at its core. People came to it from different places for different reasons, but an allergic reaction to convention was its center, music was the soundtrack and its influence continued to grow.

When songwriters of that serious perspective and social consciousness found an audience hungry for music that gave them a voice, an anthem, a gathering place to share the experience, the classic era of rock & roll quickly came to be. It began to completely reshape the music business. It also took a very big swing at reshaping society itself.

There was a hipster tradition celebrated in the happening literature of the time, artists experimenting with new ways of painting, photographing, and filming, even one day in the near future draping mountain canyons with fabric, a small, devoted audience for folk and protest music, and the pathway for a signal change in the social fabric, when all those cultural expressions of the outliers suddenly became marginally mainstream and classic rock & roll came thundering into the Rockies.

A SKY LARK
RECORDING
33 1/2 HI-FI

FOLK SONG
FESTIVAL AT
EXODUS
GALLERY BAR

DENVER
COLORADO

featuring
WALT CONLEY
JUDY COLLINS

3

BIG GUITAR

THE EXODUS ON LINCOLN STREET was the premiere club for folk music in Denver. Hal Neustaedter ran it and everybody played there. Locals like Judy Collins and Walt Conley, stalwarts like Doc Watson, Phil Ochs, Dave Van Ronk, Odetta, Josh White, and more mainstream acts like the New Christy Minstrels, the Chad Mitchell Trio, the Smothers Brothers, and the Kingston Trio.

He never made the Exodus stage, but there was even a young and very ragged hustler who was scrambling from one open mike to another all over town, learning how to be a folksinger from anyone who would give him the time of day, developing the persona that would become, writ large, Bob Dylan.

Legend has it that Conley got Dylan his first paying gig that summer of 1960 at the Gilded Garter in Central City, mainly as a way of getting him out of town because nobody much cared for his scruffy act. Four years later, he packed them in at the Denver Auditorium and everywhere else he played. The rest, as they say...

Maybe you worked a few doors up 20th Avenue from the Exodus, washing dishes and hanging out at Les Tarot, a quintessential coffee house owned by Merlin and Taggart Dyke, refugees from the New York theater scene who kept a bizarre collection of stage props and costumes in the basement. They hosted most of the city's Beats and folkies, who gathered around one of the Rocky Mountain area's two grandiose Venetian espresso machines for poetry readings, chess, multiple cups of coffee and too many cigarettes, quiet contemplation and endless discussions about literature, music, and what it was that was truly hip.

Up the street on 17th Avenue a few more blocks south and east was the Green Spider, run by Don Lehn, another coffeehouse favored by the folkies and Beats, as was the Satire Lounge on Colfax, another few blocks further in the same direction, where stronger brew was served and Walt Conley for many years held sway.

In 1962, immediately next door to the Spider, a guitar-playing kid from Philadelphia named Harry Tuft opened the Denver Folklore Center, which quickly became the hub of the music scene. Dylan had his mail forwarded there. Pete Seeger, Joan Baez, Earl Scruggs, Ramblin' Jack Elliott, and nearly every other big name of that era passed through its doors. All the local players treated it like the General Store. Whatever the level of your talent, flat out professional or just a wannabe, the Folklore Center was the place to be.

Everybody bought their strings and picks there, sheet music and blues albums, and when they had the bucks, maybe they finally sprung for a very fine old Martin D28 or a beautiful new Guild to make those especially sweet sounds. Harry and his team taught a legion of folkies finger picking, standard Pete Seeger and Woody Guthrie, old union strike songs and deep South blues tunes, and probably put up more than a few of these fledgling bohemians for a night around the old wood stove in the back of the store when the snow was flying and the streets were cold.

Harry would become the first important concert promoter of our time for music outside the mainstream, putting on shows by the Seekers, Judy Collins, and, in a burst of promotion in 1966, Flat & Scruggs, Ian & Sylvia, Ravi Shankar, and Charles Lloyd at the Auditorium Theater, as well as later dates with Pete Seeger and Arlo Guthrie, and then Joan Baez at Red Rocks. In time, his work promoting music would lead to the formation of Swallow Hill Music. He also was the guy who helped a kid from Chicago named Barry Fey make the transition from booking acts to promoting shows. That was later.

So, Hal Neustaedter and his club scene in a sense begat Harry Tuft and his Auditorium Arena shows. One day soon, Barry Fey and his stadium shows would beget Chuck Morris and his prominence in the concert scene nationwide. You just happened to be there and see it take place from close by. It wasn't your intention, really, but just timing and curiosity that led you there. That's the end of this story, though, and you're now barely at the beginning.

Maybe you knew the Tarot better than the others because you worked there, but all those places had a magnetic attraction, hip, mysterious and enchanting. Something was happening here and you wanted to know what it was. It was new and different from everything else. You spent nearly every night in one or another of those places, cruising 17th Avenue, Sherman, Grant and Lincoln, easing through the shadows, awestruck and hungry for more.

So, only 14 and for years thereafter, you snuck in the back door of the Exodus, through the funky kitchen past the wooden paddles stacked with greasy sandwiches, the stout glass pitchers of beer, and on down the stairs to the Catacombs, to watch Carolyn Hester, or Tom Paxton, or George Carlin, or to gaze in awe at the gorgeous singer in the little black dress with great legs, a big guitar and hellacious pipes whose name was Judy Roderick, and who later came to rock & roll as lead singer for 60,000,000 Buffalo and Big Sky Mud Flaps.

Many a folksinger would make that transition, but rock & roll for now was kid's stuff. Like sugar addicts, we still took long, shaky sips of pop music, but payola was taking its toll and the quality of the music was suffering. So, all of a sudden, here you were in high school and folk music was for serious people, those of us who were growing up.

A day would come when the Esplanade at East High School, the very same place that many mornings featured drag races between the hottest '55 Chevy on the street and the '57 Ford with the T-Bird engine under the hood, both of them laying rubber from the Circle to nearly where they had to back off at the traffic light on 17th Avenue or plunge through the intersection into City Park; in that very same place, there came a day when Mac Ferris and Judy Evans would stretch out on the lawn there, strumming and singing plaintive songs of the downtrodden while crowds of kids, mostly white folks at a time when the Crayola box you grew up with had a color named Flesh and it was pink, as if describing the many from the Country Club neighborhood from just south of school who would ponder the truth of it all.

East High School, Home of the Angels

A GIRL DELINQUENT...
A JET PROPELLED GANG...
OUT FOR FAST KICKS!

JUVENILE JUNGLE

in NATURAMA

STARRING
COREY ALLEN · REBECCA WELLES
RICHARD BAKALYAN
ANNE WHITFIELD · JOE DI REDA
with
JOE CONLEY · WALTER COY · TAGGART CASEY
HUGH LAWRENCE · LEON TYLER · HARVEY GRANT

Produced by SIDNEY PICKER · Directed by WILLIAM WITNEY · Written by ARTHUR T. HORMAN · REPUBLIC PICTURES Presents A CORONADO Production

4

UNTAMED YOUTH

THERE WERE A COUPLE OF DOZEN RADIO STATIONS in Denver in the Fifties and into the Sixties, all of them that we knew about on the AM band because that's all most radios could play. One of them, 95 KIMN, for many years owned more than a quarter of the total audience in town, and for one brief time in the Fifties claimed a 56 share.

It was the quintessential top 40 station, playing (and making) one hit after another. The disc jockeys were local celebrities: Steve Kelley, Jay Mack, Roy the Bell Boy Gunderson, and the eponymous Pogo Poge (aka Morgan White). They knew how to keep the music coming and they knew how to promote.

Poge got his name by riding a pogo stick all the way to Boulder in the days when that was a long and lonely road. He broadcast his show several different times with maximum promotion from behind a glass-walled snake pit on a street corner downtown in the Zale's Jewelers on 16th Street, even managing to get bitten one time, which only added to his reputation.

So the crowds of teenagers filed past, while pythons slithered and rattlers rattled and cobras vented their mighty hoods, and Pogo kept spinning the records. Roy Orbison, Chuck Berry, the Everly Brothers, Little Richard, Buddy Holly, and Jerry Lee Lewis wailed away through the speakers hung on the wall outside. Who wouldn't love it? 56 percent of us in Denver did.

Stylin' on the East Coast

It was a time that celebrated juvenile delinquents, The Wild Ones, The Blackboard Jungle, James Dean. Bill Haley and the Comets. Rock Around the Clock. Jailhouse Rock. You were a Soc or a Greaser, no ethnicity implied. The clean cut kids wore white shirts, khakis and loafers. The guys with ducktails turned out in black t-shirts and Levis with motorcycle boots, a deck of Luckies neatly rolled up in one sleeve above a bulging bicep. That was stylin'.

There were locally legendary characters who fought their way to fame, guys like Abe Stongel in Globeville, Bob Seegmiller in South Denver, and later Paul Landauer and his brothers in Park Hill. There were tough kids all over town. If you spent a night at Juvie, after Judge Gilliam lectured you about heading in the wrong direction and giving you a taste of what awaited you if you didn't straighten up, you had some street cred. The really bad guys went away to Lookout Mountain for a stretch.

Until they were old enough to motor, kids needed a place to hang out. Neighborhood soda fountains at the drugstores were popular afternoons and movie theaters like the Tower on 23rd and Krameria were where you wanted to be at night. It was near Blood Alley, a famed place for fights, and was haunted by two notorious motorcycle cops, Buster Snider and J.D. Wilkerson, who for many years made their chops riding herd on teenagers in Denver.

Sock hops and socials were the places you gathered when you could. The Methodist Church on Montview and Glencoe used to put on a pretty good show in a big basement room once a month or so. Kids from all over the east side and elsewhere, too, all of you would show up to dance your ass off to really good tunes, the Everly Brothers, Bo Diddley, Carl Perkins, Little Richard, Ricky Nelson, Gene Vincent, the Big Bopper, Eddie Cochran, Chuck Berry, and, of course, Elvis. Whoever chose the music there was really good and you made it every chance you could. It was worth a long bike ride on a cold night to get your yayas out.

Friday and Saturday nights, you knew just enough girls whose parents thought it was enlightened to have all their post-pubescent pals over for quiet, that is, unsupervised, gatherings in the rec rooms of their generous homes. You and Mike O'Shea would ride your bikes all the way from 32nd Avenue to Alameda and Monaco, where Kathy Nevin and her folks lived in a big old house set back off the road. Some times it was so cold, your hands would be frozen and your teeth chattering when you arrived. But it was worth it.

Sock Hops and Saddle Shoes 1959

The music was quieter. Paul Anka's "Put Your Head on My Shoulder" (Whisper in my ear, baby, words I want to hear, maybe), "Sea of Love" by the Honeydrippers (Come with me, my love, to the sea, the sea of love), "I Only Have Eyes For You" by the Flamingos (You are here, sha bop, and so am I), that sort of stuff. The purpose was making out, duh! Seeing just how far the mood could take you, slow dancing pubic bone to pubic bone, lips locked together, and later sprawling on sofas, hands everywhere. The scent of hormonal rage wafting through the room.

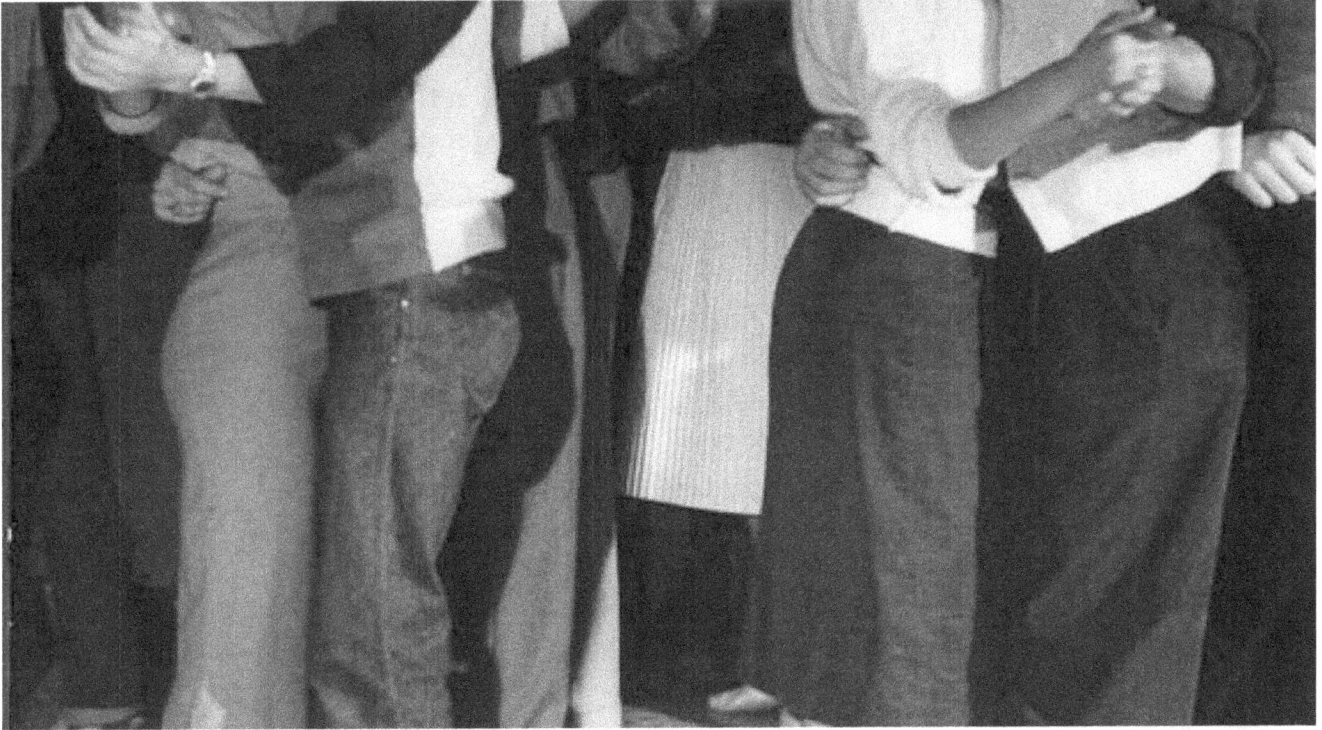

At just the right moment, Johnny Mathis would launch into "It's Not for Me to Say", and before the song was over, you would get absolutely as far down the road as you were gonna get that night. Maybe as far as you ever dared in your best dream. Perhaps the glow of love will grow. Something like that. On the long ride home in the freezing night, pedaling furiously, you were so hot and bothered steam would be rising off you in clouds.

Once you were old enough to drive, or had friends who were willing to give you a ride, you really started to get around. In style. Hoppin' and boppin'. All the while, the radio blasting those great Top 40 tunes. The Ronettes, the Shirelles, the Orions, Martha and the Vandellas, the Cookies.

New learning experiences awaited you. Like speed traps. Glendale was one. That little independent municipality on the east side of Colorado Boulevard between Alameda and somewhere further south, Jewell Avenue or thereabouts.

There was no way to get to Celebrity Lanes or the first McDonald's in town on Mississippi Avenue, without traveling that scary stretch of road. Blink and you're busted. A township that supported itself with speeding tickets. And kids in cars were ripe pickings. So you'd get a Big Mac with your pals and all of you but especially the driver would hold your breath as you headed north down the hill through Glendale. When Bob's Cowboy Drive-In, a gas station of sorts just shy of Alameda, came into view, you could begin to exhale and live to ride another day.

If you lived on the North side, you went to the Scotchman Drive-In, where the cars lined up down the block on Federal Friday and Saturday nights, waiting to get in. On the East side, the Holiday Drive-In (the Lid, the East Lid on Colfax, the South Lid on Colorado Boulevard) was the place to see and be seen. Maybe you had a run in with Buster Snider one night, who handcuffed you to a pole at the far end of the runway at the East Lid where all the cars parked and the car hops served them, and in the course of a few hours chained to that spot, you saw nearly everybody you knew in town as they circled through the parking lot. Most all of them had something to say to you, too, yelled out the open window with the music wailing in the background as they slowly drove by, laughing.

5

THEATER

ANOTHER MAJOR ENTERTAINMENT VENUE in the day was the movie theater. Way before the multiplex came to anchor shopping centers everywhere, extraordinary buildings seating several thousand in luxury unimaginable today were a fixture of every city's downtown. The Boulder Theatre, a magnificent facility built in the grand, ornate, and acoustically perfect style of the Twenties and Thirties, one day would become a concert hall where bands took advantage of a stage built for a full sized concert orchestra to ply its wares. Before that, it was just another theater.

In Denver, these places existed by the dozens: the Centre, the Denham, the Isis, the Aladdin, the Mayan, the Victory, the Bluebird, the Federal, the Ogden, the Esquire, and on and on. Thankfully, a number of the smaller ones have survived, although in crudely partitioned form. Of the very large ones, those that seated thousands, only the Paramount remains today. It has hosted some extraordinary concerts in the years since it was salvaged from the wrecker's ball.

They would run a film for weeks on end and fill the theater night after night. Television increasingly over time put a dent in attendance, and little by little developers came to see more profitable uses for the real estate. If you ever had the pleasure of sitting in one of those beautiful theaters, having entered through any of the multiple brass doors under the huge marquee, through the grandiose lobby with its brilliantly lit concession stands, maybe climbed the grand stairway winding up to the balcony, settled back in the plush seats, wrapped in walls of elaborate deco designs with sconces for lighting, gracefully curved brass railings, and thick curtains of plush velvet perhaps 40 x 100 feet in size that opened to reveal a screen built for Hollywood's stream of fantasies played out in Cinemascope and VistaVision; if you and many hundreds of others sitting there together failed to realize how rare and soon to disappear that movie-going experience was, you can hardly be blamed. Who could imagine buildings that beautiful would soon be destroyed so department stores and Walgreens could replace them in the relentless march of commerce?

Few of them were still standing by the time the golden age of film in the Seventies arrived. But where we could, in smaller groups, we gathered to see The Godfather, Chinatown, Apocalypse Now, The Deer Hunter, One Flew Over the Cuckoo's Nest, The French Connection, A Clockwork Orange, films that rank among the greatest ever made. Like that time in music, it was an era of brilliant filmmaking driven by a brief respite from corporate dominance of the business.

Maybe you saw Patton on your 25th birthday. Someone kindly gave you a handful of mescaline as a present just as you left for the theater. Before the film began, you reached in your pocket and grabbed a few of the tabs. The first one hadn't yet taken effect as the movie started and George C. Scott appeared on the screen before an American flag the size of a football field. Unconsciously, you began to gobble up those powerful little pills into your mouth like popcorn, transfixed by the spectacle on the screen. More than a few had entered your bloodstream by the time you realized what you'd done. It was literally dazzling. Patton, the story of that troubled poet-warrior, ever since has seemed to you perhaps the greatest movie ever made. Well, sorta.

Drive-In theaters, too, by then were coming to the end of their time as a place where people gathered. For a long time, they had served as somewhat sheltered places for teenagers, where you could spend an evening making out, and maybe more, in the relative privacy of your car. It wasn't uncommon for groups of kids to ride in the trunk past the admissions stand, where a single driver or, less suspiciously, maybe a couple bought their tickets and, once safely inside, somewhere in a back row, they'd open the trunk and their friends would emerge to watch the show for free. Daylight savings time put a serious dent in the business, and changing times of the social sort eroded attendance. Maybe all those free tickets did some damage, too.

Frankie and Annette making teen

6

BABY WON'T YOU BOP?

IN THE FIFTIES IN DENVER, there wasn't much live rock & roll. But little by little it started coming on. The great Gene Vincent and the Blue Caps, hep cats to the nth degree, played a downtown roller rink in maybe 1958. People called them rockabilly, but they may have been the first punk band. Gene had a blatantly erotic way with phrasing his songs. There was a lot of 'uckin' in the way he sang "hugging and kissing and loving all night," which buried his career on radio.

But, for now, he was raging. You'd never seen anything like it. Not in person, for sure. Cliff Gallup was maybe the best lead guitar player of his time. Between them, they generated a lot of heat. At one point in the show, a couple of the Blue Caps slid up and down Gene's body while they wailed away on a very hot version of "Be-Bop-A Lula," and people began walking out in droves. This was *not* how Pat Boone did it. But maybe you were one of the ones with your mouth hanging open, your heart pounding, jumping up and down, boppin' the blues. Your first live rock & roll show and not a bad place to start.

Most of the live music was made by local bands at 3.2 clubs all over town. Teenagers 18 and over, and a whole lot of younger ones with fake IDs, gathered in the clubs that served low alcohol beer and a whole lot of hellraising.

Katz Korner on East Colfax was more famous for its brawlers than its music. The best known was Tom Traubert, whom singer/songwriter Tom Waits immortalized some years after Traubert was stabbed to death in a school yard at 12th and Acoma. Waits said that he "was a friend of a friend," that friend being the equally celebrated Chuck E. Weiss, a notorious character in East Denver long before he gained a measure of fame with his band The Goddamn Liars in Los Angeles and long before Ricky Lee Jones told us "Chuck E.'s In Love."

Maybe you walked down a street in Park Hill in the years even before we were teenagers and saw on a big white, doublewide garage door, writ large in black paint:

Fuck Twice Chuck Weiss. That was the story. Don't know if it's true. He was famous in Denver before he was 12. His brother, Wizzy, ran the Record Center downtown, which was the place where everybody bought those 45s we heard on KIMN. Chuck E. knew his music from a very early age and made it work for him.

There were bands all over the Front Range, working the Red Garter in Ft. Collins, Sam's on Lookout Mountain, the Red Room on Federal in Thornton, the Honeycomb in Aurora, the Cave in Littleton, about a dozen in the Springs, most famously the Hallabaloo on North Nevada, and in Pueblo, The Honeybucket, the Hi-Fi, and Pinocchio's, where Tony Spicola held sway. They went by names like the Status Seekers, Gary Stites and the Satellites, the Stonebreakers, and the Sting Rays just to breeze through the Ss; the Brambles, the Checkmates, the Viscounts, the Fogcutters, the Monocles, King Louie and the Laymen, the Vaqueros, and the Leather Souls.

There were dozens, maybe hundreds more, playing wherever they could, at parties, sock hops, keggers, woodsies, weddings, bar mitzvahs, most of them hoping for the big time, which meant a paying gig at a 3.2 club and, who knows, maybe even a record contract to cut a 45? Several of them did, but most just faded away or morphed into other bands. A few of those musicians found fame and fortune with one band or another. Most of them just had fun.

In Denver, the music scene at clubs was thriving. Out by DU on Buchtel Boulevard was the Crimson and Gold, which catered to the college crowd. There were a couple of places on Santa Fe Drive, the famed La Pichet (the Pitcher) on West Mississippi, the Posh on West Evans, and way out on Colfax in Lakewood, the Lemon Tree Lounge. Maybe the best of them all was a place on Alameda Avenue just shy of Sheridan that really rocked, the Galaxy.

A group called the Soul Survivors, led by Allen Kemp, Pat Shanahan, and Gene Chalk, was the house band for many years. Allen and Pat made it big, first as the Stone Canyon Band, which backed Rick Nelson at the peak of his career, and later as The New Riders of the Purple Sage. Another Survivor, bassist Bob Raymond, was later a member of Sugarloaf.

The big band in Denver, though, was the Moonrakers. Denny Flannigan, Joel Brandes, Veeder Van Dorn, and the Bobs, MacVittie and Webber, rocked the best fraternity parties in town and played the big venues like the Trocadero at Elitch's and Club Baja downtown. They had a huge hit with "I'm All Right" and a series of great tunes that carried them through to the hippie days when some of them formed Chocolate Hair, which soon thereafter became Sugarloaf.

The Moonrakers early 1960s

The really hip teenagers in Denver carried their fake IDs to Boulder, where Stormy Patterson and the Storm Troopers were the house band at the Olympic Lounge, a bowling alley and dance club out in the sticks near where 30th Street is today. Maybe you were one of the legions of teens who drove the Boulder Toll Road, all 27 miles through the empty fields in the pitch black night, paid the 25 cent toll at the little booth in the middle of nowhere where eventually the City and County of Broomfield came to be, and finally reached the Olympic, where you'd drink dollar pitchers of beer all night and shake your bootie to really great tunes with the cutest girls you knew until midnight finally came, the club closed down, and you made the long, drunken drive back to Denver.

Boulder, too, was Tulagi's, where the best known (and maybe the best) local band of those days, the Astronauts, held forth. They and the Moonrakers had many a Battle of the Bands, vying for supremacy in the competition for fraternity party gigs, graduation parties, and all the other rituals of teenage life that increasingly centered around rock & roll. Who knew you could make a few bucks doing this stuff?

Maybe you crashed a party or two at the notorious Beta House on the Hill, a precursor to Animal House by a decade or better. The Astronauts played in the main room downstairs where those still standing twisted the night away, hallways were littered with bodies mostly or totally drunk, bedrooms with bodies partly or nearly naked, and inebriated bikers rode their motorcycles up the main stairway to the second or third floors, just because they could.

CU was a famous party school in those days. Playboy Magazine, which mattered back then, for several years running named it the Number 1 campus in the country for flat out, party-hearty atmosphere. The fact you could drink beer at 18 probably had a lot to do with it.

Boulder itself was dry. You had to go up the canyon to the Red Lion Inn, where Chris and Heidi Mueller served many a famous party or two, or east past 24th on Arapahoe (the city limit then) to the Lamp Post, if you wanted a real drink. Partying hard and being famous for it was a source of pride for the kids, 3.2 beer was the juice, and a lot of us took it very seriously. You had a job to do in building a reputation to uphold.

They checked IDs a little closer at Tulagi's than most of the other joints, but if yours came from Fuller and Chew, those enterprising boys from East High, you probably would pass. You could hole up inside that sandstone building on the Hill and rock out all night to Rich Fifield and the band. Stormy had joined them by then on bass, Jimmy Gallagher was the drummer, Bob Demmon and Dennis Lindsey were the rest of the rhythm section. They packed 'em in night after night.

The excitement that built around the contract they signed to "cut a record" in L.A. turned to skepticism when it came out as "Surfin' With The Astronauts." In the era of the Beach Boys, it perhaps was inevitable, but this was your music, not California. If you could get past the Rocky Mountain surfer aspect, though, it was a pretty damned good album, the first of many they made.

credit: Carnegie Library for Local History

Down the Hill at the end of the block was The Sink, where Herb Kauvar held forth for many years, and you hadn't lived until you'd had a Sink Burger. The walls were covered with caricatures by Llloyd (three "l's" just because) Kavich, a local Beat artist, behind the counter a wide-eyed kid named Chuck Morris poured cheap pitchers of Coors, and a redheaded student with a big future ahead of him named Robert Redford mopped the floor.

Cater-corner across 13th in the basement of a wedge-shaped building, beneath a bicycle shop, was the Attic, where soon to be famous rockers like David Crosby, Roger McGuinn and Chris Hillman separately plied their plaintive folk songs to college kids. Everybody who was nobody played there, but some of them became somebody after a while.

Further down, at Broadway and Arapahoe Street, was the Gondolier, a pizza joint owned by Gary and Warren, whose last names escape your memory, that fed many an inebriated teenager and sobered

them up with coffee from the other great Venetian Espresso machine, an exact match to the one at the Tarot. There were very few places in Boulder, other than the 3.2 joints, that stayed open past 10 p.m. The Gondolier and the Donut Hole downtown were just about it. It was pizza and coffee or donuts and coffee, your choice.

Someday you would be a dropout riding motorcycles and gathering for FAC at The Sink with every other biker in town. Howard Higman, a sociology professor at CU who founded the World Affairs Conference with Betty Weems, would pass around paper sacks full of peyote buttons with instructions for preparing them and a questionnaire to be returned to him elucidating the effects of your trip.

You'd ride your bike back to the apartment near the Doozy Duds, the Laundromat where everybody washed their dirty clothes once or twice a month when they finally became unwieldy, park your ferocious Triumph 650 or maybe your Bonneville, your Norton, or your BSA 441 Victor where you kept it in the living room, heat up the oven, and cook up a batch of hallucinogenics to trip the night away.

The first bust in Boulder those days happened at 711 Pearl, which was said to involve explosives as much as drugs. It was something of a surprise. There would come a time a few years hence, maybe 1967 or so, when people were selling bales of pot from the back of pickup trucks parked on the Hill and nobody seemed to mind.

The salad days came to an abrupt end when it was claimed the Weathermen (to know which way the wind blows) exploded a bomb in Mackie Auditorium. Federal agents came to town to investigate the bombing, took one look around and said to themselves, "What the fuck is going on here?" Thereafter, everything changed again and everyday life in Boulder came under more scrutiny.

But that was to come later. For now, it was still a time of innocence and wonder. Everything was uncertain and anything seemed possible.

7

---

20 YEARS OF SCHOOLIN'

FOLK MUSIC LASTED FOR A WEEK AND A DAY, or so it seemed. Everyone was earnest, wore denim and sandals, everyone made a point of getting to know a Negro (not all of whom were necessarily interested in getting known, thank your honky ass so much), Young People's Socialist Leaguers (can you say: Yipsels?) in their denim shirts, jeans and sandals, their long, unkempt hair and beards were a hint of what was coming. The times they were a changin' and the YPSLs dug it. So did a lot of other folks, but some of 'em wanted more.

Maybe you thought to yourself the music was okay, all this serious stuff about "A Hard Rain" and "Talkin' John Birch Paranoid Blues," a lot to ruminate about and it almost kept you awake but it just might be better if they added some drums. And one bright, sunny day you were walking down the Hill, past Bennett's Pizza and Subs, opposite Kinsley & Co., where madras shirts and blazers hung in the windows, just listening to your transistor radio, and on came "Subterranean Homesick Blues." (Look out kid, it's something you did, god knows when but you're doing it again). And, from that moment forward, you wanted to keep on doing it. (Jump down the manhole, light yourself a candle, don't wear sandals, try to avoid the scandals). Works for you!

At the Newport Folk Festival, Pete Seeger was trying to take an ax to the power cable, but there was no silencing Bob Dylan and no stopping the next iteration of rock & roll. Pete overnight became an antique.

Then came the Beatles and the British invasion, and before you could begin to get a handle on that, here came psychedelia. Don't you want somebody to love? Don't you need somebody to love? You better find somebody to love. Yeah! 1967 and the Summer of Love. Flower power. Watch your head, Head!

You were a blue-collar kid, not very keen on school, saw it as part of the propaganda mill. Went to register at CU and stood in a line at the Fieldhouse with 20 or 30,000 other schlubs. Where you would learn to be an individual, right? Stand on your own, think for yourself? Maybe you had better things to do.

College wasn't automatic for the kids in your neighborhood. Some people you knew, the ones in Park Hill, Congress Park, the Country Club, and Hilltop, there was no question. Just a matter of where, not if. Not so where you came from. Guys you knew wanted to get a job right out of high school, start making some money, buy a car, beers at the bar after work with the boys, sooner or later knock up your girlfriend and finally settle down. At 20 or 21. If not sooner.

A lot of the guys from the 'hood became cops. You knew a bunch of them. Older brothers of guys at school. They had their eye on you. Thought you might be a guy to bring around. Talked you up to each other. Talked up the life to you. How it worked. What it was. Urban cowboys is what they were. Riding herd. They took you places, showed you things. You knew it wasn't for you, but they didn't know it yet. So, they laid it on thick. Cops have groupies, too, you know. And articles about them in the papers. You get the good gigs if you're in the loop. Free meals and booze, tickets to the games. Security for big events when they come to town. Better than front row seats.

So, the Beatles played Red Rocks in 1964. Tickets were $6 and it didn't sell out. The band stayed at the Brown Palace and maybe you rode an elevator with John Lennon, who said "Hullo" and looked amused. At the show, you stood in the wings stage right and the sound was deafening – not the band but the screaming fans, who drowned out whatever noise the Beatles were making. The concert lasted barely an hour, but your ears rang for days. And it got better.

12 X 5 by the Rolling Stones was the album everybody danced to at parties in apartments all over Boulder. The live band of the moment, maybe another contender for the country's very first punk rockers, was the Leopold Fuchs Hate Band. Mac Ferris, Holly Cotton, Sam Appleton, Lenny Lookner, all these rich kids from back East who lived in a biker pad out by 30th street, which was way out in the country then.

They were said to appropriate motorcycles belonging to others that they carried off in a van and converted to someone else's property when no one was looking. You doubt that it was true but it added to their legend. They always treated you very well, helped you keep the Triumph running, joined you gooning the sudden emergence of coeds riding little Moped-like Honda 50s. Japanese bikes were to laugh at, right? Who could have guessed what was to come?

The Fuchs played pretty good music, too. Some of them later went up to Aspen and ran Galena Street East, where many a newly formed Colorado band found a stage to perform. One of them was Brown Sugar, led by Candy and David Givens, who migrated to Boulder, met a kid from American Standard by the name of Tommy Bolin, and Zephyr was born. But that was later, too.

Bob Dylan and the Beatles blew up the music business. Tin Pan Alley never recovered.

Lennon-McCartney, the Glimmer Twins, Elton John and Bernie Taupin, Carole King, Joni Mitchell, Simon and Garfunkel, hundreds more after them. They wrote and performed their music. Before long, they began to produce it, too. Then, they learned the business and cut deals to distribute it end to end. The power flowed to the artist and away from the suits who always before held sway. Own the songbook, you were king, or queen.

That was one of three things that set the stage. The other two were the emergence of FM radio, and the corresponding development of the record album over 45s as the packaging medium of choice. Or vice versa. It was symbiotic.

Music now was the province of the singer/songwriter, and the influence they exerted would change the business permanently. There are plenty of great players, but not a lot of great writers. The few who are one in the same gathered great influence, wealth, and power. They also opened up the door for a lot of others to at least give it a try. The result was an absolutely staggering and unprecedented period of creativity.

All this is prelude to the explosion. The first rumblings. There was stuff going on in Colorado that provided the powder. Some infrastructure, a little tradition, certifiable characters looming large, and a bunch of good musicians either locally born or gathering from elsewhere.

Maybe you met Mick Durbin one day, driving the first Ford Mustang that hit town midway in 1964 and playing a pretty mean folk guitar, which in a couple of years turned into a pretty mean rock guitar. Mick was in and out of bands in Denver, Boulder and Aspen, and he seemed to know everybody, including you. He had a way with music and a way with the ladies, one of whom, the sublime, extraordinary, chain-smoking Joni Mitchell, would say so in a song called "Michael From Mountains," one of her hundred or so best tunes.

Mick knew Jeff Cook, who knew Kenny Passarelli, who knew Mac Ferris, who knew George Grantham. Otis Taylor was younger but eventually he was in there, too.

He one day would win many awards for his interpretation of the blues, but now he was just another kid in the mix. It built like that. They were all just kids then, feeling their way, inspired by Elvis and Dylan and the Beatles and the Stones, all these exotic cats who made that magic music and these kids wanted to make it, too. It took a while before the stars aligned, but when they did, the kids were alright and they were ready.

There was a passion that swept the Brits when they first heard American rhythm & blues and a corresponding passion that swept the U.S. in response to the British invasion. Mods and Rockers. Carnaby Street. Twiggie. Blow Up. Beatles, Stones, The Who, the Yardbirds. For a couple of years, it was all you heard and all you wanted to hear. But a response was bubbling up all over the States, colloquially at first and then increasingly communally.

The Yardbirds mid-Sixties, with both Jeff Beck and Jimmy Page

Old School

8

CAPISCE?

S O, MAYBE YOU WENT OFF TO NEW YORK For a while, where the Diggers were living in a commune on East 11th in the Village and feeding people from food carts on the streets for free every afternoon; where very strange bands like your friend John Weisenthal's Soft White Underbelly were opening for even stranger bands at the Balloon Farm, once called the Dom and later the Electric Circus, where Andy Warhol and his folks held forth before there was the Factory. The Village Theater, which was to become the Fillmore East, and Café Au Go Go, where Lenny Bruce a few years earlier had been dragged off stage and arrested, and where Sandy Phelps recalls a show that Judy Roderick headlined one night, backed by Artie Traum, with the opening act being John Hammond, Jr. backed by Jimmy James and the Blue Flames. The guitarist played with his teeth and actually spelled his name, Jimi. Tells you just how good Judy really was that she and Artie held the house that night. Just thinking about it is a rush. Here and in a thousand other venues, rock & roll was taking hold.

There were concerts in Washington Square and concerts in Central Park and a strange Asian woman named Yoko was beheading a rooster and spraying the audience with its blood at St. Mark's church, while out at Stony Brook more Happenings were held weekly and people were gathering.

You met a guy named Michael Mitchell, a painter in Westport who knew everybody, it seemed. Invited you to parties. There was Robert Rauschenberg, there was Jasper Johns (never heard of either one of them). Another guy told you that his name was Robert Nevada, but he changed it to Indiana because it was more melodious and mid-Western. Hard to know who to believe.

There was Milton Glaser. You had heard of him because your friend, Randy Enos, who began the trend of cartoon characters with vacant eyeballs, an apt illustration of the times, and designed the Tonight Show logo (tonight, tonight, tonight in puffs from the chimney as the train rolls past) did some work for Push Pin Studios in the City, where Glaser did the psychedelic, spaghetti-haired poster of Bob Dylan, not to mention the I (heart) NY graphic, and lots of other cutting edge graphic design.

Randy was an unusual looking guy with a very flamboyant way of dressing. One day in Manhattan, you were meeting him for lunch. He came strolling down the street in a rather vivid purple suit with polka dot tie and dapper straw hat. Coming the opposite way was Tom Wolfe in a similar straw hat, cream colored suit and tie, starched shirt, and spats. They passed each other amidst the throngs of New Yorkers on the sidewalk and each of them walked on about ten yards or so; then, simultaneously, they stopped, turned around, and had a good look at the other. A slight smile, a nod of the head, and they moved on.

One night, at one lower East Side gathering, amidst all these glamorous people, there was Veruschka, one of the first super models. Her, you had heard of. Yow! You were the same height, and born the same day of the year, but she was a lot better looking. A whole lot richer and more famous, too.

Truth be told, much as you loved rock & roll, and liked folk music pretty well, especially the blues, it was jazz that really moved you. Walking down a street in the Village, hearing an incredible sound pouring forth from a club, you walk in to a room, no cover charge asked with maybe 30 people sitting around and Miles Davis playing with his back to the room.

In the previous few years, you'd literally worn the grooves out of your first copy of Sketches of Spain, and Kind of Blue is an album you've played maybe more than any other in your lifetime. Miles live was another experience all together and the first of several times over the years you would have the pleasure.

There was an evening, too, when a cat you knew in New Jersey got you a gig with him parking cars at a club in Cherry Hill. All these goombahs in their Cadillacs and Continentals, wives or whomever in diamonds and furs, would pull up to the valet stand, hand you the keys, look at you with very serious intent, and say, "Not even one scratch, huh! Or I'll hurt you." And hand you five bucks for your trouble.

The act that night was a singer formerly from Hoboken who packed the place in a heartbeat. When the cars were parked and the show began, you and your pal stood inside the back door in the dark with a perfect view of the stage, where Frank Sinatra sang for nearly two hours and, as he always did, blew the room away. There are critics who have said of him that his voice made sounds no other singer has ever made. The Chairman of the Board was a phenomenon.

The old crooners like Sinatra were in a class by themselves. Popular music passed them by when rock came along, but they never lost the magic. Decades later, on his Unplugged tour, Tony Bennett played the Paramount Theater in the days when the estimable Jim Sprinkle was running the non-profit side of that enterprise. You had front row seats. On one side, the guy with the diamond pinkie ring and the gal in furs with a big beehive hairdo, and on the other side, a liberally pierced and tattooed couple in matching Slayer shirts.

At one point, honoring the title of the show, Bennett signaled the sound man to turn off the mics. To the accompaniment of the great Ralph Sharon, his longtime pianist who retired to Boulder in 2002 and lived there until his death in 2015, Bennett filled every corner of that 2,200 seat room with a voice other singers can only dream of. It was absolutely stunning.

There is a story about Sinatra and Bennett ruminating one night over drinks about why their careers had prospered through all the ups and downs of the entertainment business, and all the changes in musical styles. The level of respect they command from musicians even today is universal. Keith Richards said recently about Lady Gaga: "A great talent. She's got it. Tony Bennett spotted her right away and you don't argue with Mr. Bennett."

Frank said to Tony, "What kept us up there all this time?" Tony replied: "We always sang the great songs." With really great voices, that is.

In a small cabin in the woods of Delaware you heard Blonde on Blonde when it was released. The very same day, on May 16, 1966, Pet Sounds by Brian Wilson was released. Like that first time with Elvis, Dylan's double album was unlike anything you'd heard before and nothing was ever quite the same again. But then, Pet Sounds was like nothing you'd ever heard from the Beach Boys, or anyone else for that matter. Clearly, something was happening here, there, and everywhere.

Suddenly, in fact, so much was happening everywhere in the country, seemingly simultaneously. You traveled east to west and everywhere you went, freaks were sprouting like mushrooms in the shade, flowers in their hair. Youth became a vast tribe, and culture became tribal. Costumes were donned, rituals evolved, a new language was spoken. At the center of it all was the music.

And the center of all that music at the moment was San Francisco. It was the Summer of Love. Haight-Ashbury. Golden Gate Park. The Avalon and the Fillmore. What emanated from the City by the Bay reached every corner of America and the English-speaking world almost overnight. How that well-known, thoroughly reported cultural phenomenon made its way to Denver, like it made its way east and west in a heartbeat, begins the later part of the story of Denver in the Sixties.

Detroit could be Anywhere USA

9

REALITY BITES

YOU CAN'T UNDERSTAND THE SIXTIES without coming to grips with these terrible truths, the reality America was living with and what its youth saw as its bequest: civil rights and urban riots, the Vietnam War and war resisters, and crude political assassinations. You wrestled with these things, day after day and year after year in trying to come of age. You wondered what it all meant and what to do about it.

It was baffling, confusing, dismaying. Maybe you felt lied to by the powers that be. Parents, teachers, coaches, priests and nuns, all the local hotshots in the business community, they all were telling you things that obviously weren't true. You'd see it in the streets and then see it on TV, or hear the official version as it made the rounds. It didn't wash. It was a belief system you couldn't believe in, a story line that didn't hold up in the face of what you knew to be true.

In a five year period in the middle of that turbulent decade, four towering national leaders were slain by assassins: John Kennedy, Malcolm X, Martin Luther King, and Bobby Kennedy. The day John Kennedy was shot in 1963, you were driving down Colorado Boulevard in your '57 Ford when the news came on the radio. You didn't even know what it meant. The entire country entered a state of suspended animation, glued to the television for the next three days until his funeral. You saw the president's head explode in slow motion over and over again. Jackie Kennedy on Air Force One in her bloodstained suit. You saw Lee Harvey Oswald shot dead by Jack Ruby in a crowd of cops and news reporters right before your eyes. Saw it again and again in endless replays. Saw the long, slow march of the horse-drawn hearse past all the dignitaries and little John-John saluting. Politics was a third world country.

You were walking down Colfax one afternoon in 1968, the day of your girlfriend Rebecca Jane's birthday, and there in the newspaper box at the corner of Pearl Street hard by the Argonaut Liquors was the Rocky Mountain News with the headline:

Kennedy Assassinated. It was déjà vu, all over again.

The continued oppression of black people, from the time of slavery, through emancipation and the Jim Crow South, the ghettos of the North, the Freedom Riders, the March on Selma, Emmett Till, the Birmingham church bombings, George Wallace, the whole, ugly spectacle of institutional racism finally brought about voices that demanded change.

So one day, your second daughter was born, this person unexpected whom you would grow to dearly love and cherish, and the very next day, no sooner had you dimly begun to come to terms with her arrival, than the most eloquent person ever to have visited your very young life was shot dead on a motel balcony in Tennessee. The Lord giveth and racists take away.

When voices like Martin Luther King and Malcolm X were silenced by assassins, black America erupted in violence and black neighborhoods burned. You grew up in a very integrated place, poor people of every color, and when your black friends looked at you with hurt, anguish, and anger, you didn't know what to say or do. Burn, baby, burn! You hated it but you understood it, too.

White merchants and white slumlords, their property was set aflame, and we all got to watch it on the nightly news until the last ember was extinguished.

In California, Cesar Chavez was making big waves in his fight for the rights of migrant farm workers and here in Denver, Corky Gonzales, a handsome and charismatic former boxer with the soul of a poet was founding the Crusade for Justice to speak up for La Raza. It is too obvious to mention that everything south of the Arkansas River (can you say: R-Kansas?) was until very recently part of Mexico. Or that the oldest towns by far in Colorado are all Latino settlements. Maybe it is more important to remind ourselves that Mexico is the largest Spanish speaking country in the world. The second largest is the United States. Chicanos were no small part of the Colorado population, but they were far too small a part of the good life to be had here. Corky set out to change that.

Poor people, all of them, black, brown, red, yellow and white, at age 18 were conscripted to fight a war nobody believed in that benefitted only the military-industrial complex and some abstract notion about preserving the world for democracy. 50,000 Americans, nearly all of them younger than 30 and many of them still teenagers, died in Viet Nam. For the Domino Theory, you were told.

Two of your brothers served, one voluntarily and one drafted. Both of them came home, unlike too many of their compatriots, but neither of them ever was the same as before and one of them really never came back at all.

Hundreds of thousands were maimed. Millions of Vietnamese were killed or injured. Nobody knew what for. When the people of America by the hundreds of thousands and millions finally rose up in protest, the country was cleaved in half. Love It or Leave It versus Love Is All You Need. Which side are you on?

That was the backdrop against which the people rose up and the music played. It would not be possible to comprehend the push for peace and love, the rejection of the norm, the critical need for a voice and the music that provided it, without grasping the full dimension of the horrors playing out in the public consciousness. If the youth of the time seemed strange, compared to what?

You can go a long way down the road to change in this country without stirring up too much trouble for yourself, wear your hair long, dress outrageously, even smoke a little dope and, especially if you're white, nobody is going to get too upset about it. But when you challenge the political system in the United States, the heavy artillery is called out and you get to look it square in the eye.

So, when Corky Gonzalez rallied his people, and Lauren Watson founded the local chapter of the Black Panthers, and when the many different iterations of the War Resisters League, when all of them rose up en masse to say, "enough!" things became a little more heated.

Iconic supporters of American traditions like the Spirit of the Wild West and My Country Right or Wrong, cowboys would come to Denver each January to the National Western Stock Show, and for entertainment between their rodeo events and getting dead drunk in the bars each night would cruise the streets of Capitol Hill looking for "hippies" to harass, often beating them up or wrestling them to the ground and cutting their long hair with sheep shears. The ever present Denver Police Department seemed to find it very entertaining.

These were culture wars, and it seemed to you as it all played out they had been precisely that — battles waged between different ways of living and breathing and being—ever since you first met the Beats and the folk music crowd, wondered at their strange ways, what drove them from the mainstream into an alternative lifestyle. It was a conscious rejection of the way you were always told things were supposed to be. People were ready and willing to fight about it. The difference was that those groups were small, marginal, enigmatic segments of the American scene. Little battles of preparation.

This Youthquake, on the other hand, was a very large portion of society, and it was growing. A lot of different social initiatives coalesced around the music, which in turn began to give voice to their passions and their politics. By then, it made sense and you no longer were surprised. So much in this world you grew up in felt bad, but there were alternatives. And they felt pretty good.

There was a governing ethos of the times: if it feels good, do it! Kids who came of age in complacent, constrained, conventional, and terribly milquetoast times had learned that if their parents warned against it, if it was said to be bad, dangerous, or beneath them, it was probably a pool worth taking a dip in, an attitude worth trying on for size, maybe a way to go forward into the beyond.

Two things opened up the taps: drugs and birth control. If you were a guy raised to think your destiny was Life in the Crystal Palace as the Man in the Gray Flannel suit, that those sorts of standards were what was meant by being a success and it scared the hell out of you, drugs were an attractive alternative to life as a Conformist. A way to open up your head, rearrange your thinking, manipulate the neurons and synapses to overcome all the indoctrination they had suffered. Fast-acting, painless, no-holds-barred access to another dimension where things were very different. Hair growing out every hole in me. Think of it!

If you were a gal with aspirations to be something other than breeding stock and a stay-at-home mother with nothing to look forward to in life but kids and more kids and the PTA and bridge club and summers at the pool with all the other sagging sisters and a couple of very stiff drinks every night with your very straight old man, who was wrapped so tight nothing could get through to him – if that's what you had to look forward to and it just didn't rattle your cage, if it just seemed logical that you were capable of more than that, a lot more, birth control changed the game in major ways. Can you say: feminism?

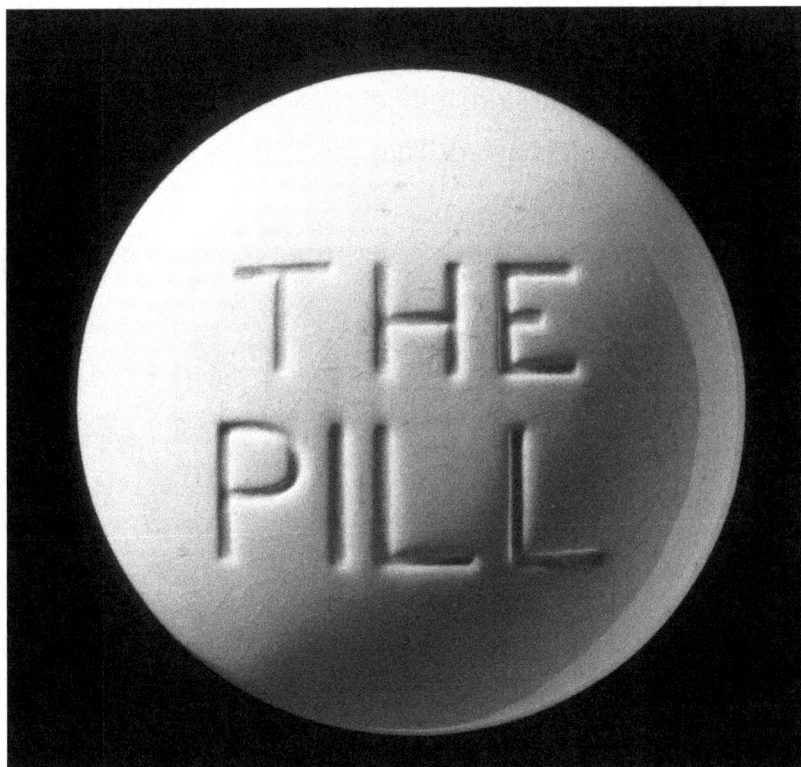

Ladies who lunch and ladies who don't, all of 'em were ready to launch into a bigger, more powerful, more meaningful, and freer role. Pregnancy hung over your head like a hatchet, ready to cleave your dreams. The specter of it ordained nearly the entirety of your sexual behavior.

The Pill was a revolution. All of a sudden you could, like, Do It! As much as you want. With anyone you want. You could beat the guys at their own game, or at least join them in it freely, maybe even without remorse. It might be great. It might be a drag. You might get off. You might get the clap. But, for the first time in the entire history of womanhood, you wouldn't get pregnant. That was a very different construct, a very visceral metaphor for freedom, and it presented a new realm of possibilities. The floodgates opened, and so did the vaginas.

Drugs, the soft ones like marijuana and hashish, and the psychedelics like mescaline, peyote, psilocybin, and especially LSD, were part and parcel of the new thing that was happening. It was all about aspiration, new ways of thinking, seeing, and doing, a reorientation of your perspective and your consciousness. "Turn on, tune in, drop out," said Tim Leary. "Go ask Alice," said Grace Slick, ""when you're 10 feet tall." "The magical mystery tour is coming to take you away," said the Fab Four. "Get high," said everyone and everything you encountered in the course of going about your day. There seemed to be a message there. What it was!

The entrenched political power had an answer: the War On Drugs and its evil twin, the Omnibus Crime Act of 1972. One of its architects, John Erlichman, who sat at the tawdry right hand of the President, Richard Nixon, later acknowledged the true intention of that vile and destructive piece of legislation: to incarcerate and deprive of their voting rights all the minorities and their supporters among the leftists of the time by making felons of them. Tie the hippies to marijuana and the blacks to heroin, he said, and let those lies do their damage. It was as cynical a piece of legislation as has ever been enacted. That was later, but it was in the works beforehand.

WHY THE WAR ON DRUG USERS?

"You want to know what this was really all about? Nixon had two enemies: the antiwar Left, and black people. **We knew we couldn't make it illegal to be either against the war or black.** But by getting the public to associate the hippies with marijuana and blacks with heroin, and then criminalizing both heavily, we could disrupt those communities. **Did we know we were lying about the drugs? Of course we did.**"

-- John Ehrlichman, Counsel and Assistant to US President Nixon

Interviewed in 1992. Full quote in "Truth, Lies, and Audiotape" (2012) by Dan Baum, journalist and author of Smoke and Mirrors: The War on Drugs and the Politics of Failure.

The War on Drugs became the cornucopia that poured forth money into every police department in the USA, and Denver was a major beneficiary. You didn't have to be the brightest bulb in the chandelier at DPD to realize that drugs were where it's at among the career paths the boys in blue could take.

The battle that ensued between the Thin Blue Line, doing its damnedest to protect the Establishment, and the counterculture assaulting the ramparts, was a very large part of the story of those times. It was a pretty easy sell. These anti-establishment types, guys with their long hair and their beards, girls with hairy armpits and unshaven legs, their braless, see through fashions with skirts so short you knew the color of their underwear (if they were wearing any), all of them with their loose morals and unapologetic licentiousness, were for most of their elders clearly subversive and revolting. What's worse, they were having fun. Fun! Singing, and dancing, and laughing. Smoking dope and having sex. The Man wanted to put a stop to it. His fat finger was on the trigger. Music was in the crosshairs.

10

FEELIN' ALRIGHT

WHEN YOU GOT BACK TO TOWN IN EARLY 1967, things were in very high gear. There were bands all over Denver and Boulder now. Some were homegrown, some were hybrids of locals and people new to town, some were altogether new. Musicians were appearing from all over the country, bringing new influences and new combinations of players, drawn to what was coming to be known as a very hip and happening place to be. It was a foretaste of the kind of migration that in the next few years would bring many a very big name musician to Colorado.

You'd go to some place one night, see a great band, people you knew, people you wanted to know, making great music together. The next night, a different place, another great band, some familiar faces and some you didn't yet know. More great music. More party. It was like that everywhere. An absolutely deafening explosion of musical creativity was sending shock waves through town and booming up and down the Front Range. And people were there in throngs, enjoying it.

That Fall, a Human Be-In held in City Park attracted tens of thousands of people, freaks of every imaginable description, to hear the Grateful Dead, Tracy Nelson and Mother Earth, Captain Beefheart, Lothar and the Hand People, and Crystal Palace Guard. Tim Leary in his formidable pre-snitch persona held forth about the joys of nature. Ken Kesey and the Merry Pranksters rolled up in that famous touring bus of theirs (We Have Come for Your Daughters), while you wandered startled and happy through the throngs of dancing, singing, brilliantly costumed people who were simply having a very good time. Stanley Owsley was there, too, which may account for the especially colorful quality of the sights and sounds.

The Family Dog had opened just a couple of weeks earlier, the Dead were in town after playing a couple of gigs there the two nights before, the newspapers and radio stations were trying to make sense of it all, many straight people were scratching their heads, and you were smiling ear to ear. What's not to like?

It was clear by then there was no turning back. This thing, this movement, this moment in time would play out over several years and effect major changes in the places and the ways we lived. You couldn't guess what it all meant, but there was a quality of unbridled joy about it that was intoxicating. And the keen sense of creativity everywhere you went was profound.

The ubiquitous Mac Ferris, Sam Fuller, brothers Kip and Tim Gilbert, and Bob Heckendorf formed the Rainy Daze (I'm savin' for the Rainy Daze), which had a huge hit with "That Acapulco Gold," written by Tim and his roommate John Carter. They also wrote a nonsense ditty called "Incense and Peppermint" that was a charter for a west coast band, The Strawberry Alarm Clock. John was later A&R man for Capitol Records in L.A. and was among the first wave of hipsters to settle in Maui. He used to send you messages that you need to come there, like, immediately, but at the time you couldn't, you were otherwise occupied. Sorry, JC.

Sam Bush and Dan Nash formed Boenzee Cryque, a band that came to feature George Grantham and Rusty Young, maybe the first guy ever to play a steel guitar in a rock band, and who later founded Poco with Richie Furay and Jim Messina. Those cross-pollinations between locals and the east and west coast musicians began the movement of big name rockers to settle in Colorado.

... **BOENZEE CRYQUE** — "It has no meaning. We picked it because it's different and phonetic."

Furay, for instance, has lived just outside Lyons for many years. Fellow Buffalo Springfield member Stephen Stills lived in the state on and off for years, and was said to have formed Crosby, Stills and Nash from jam sessions held in Mike Sterling's cabin on Flagstaff Mountain just below Twin Sisters, where you also had the pleasure of living for a couple of years, and often when the breeze rustled through the aspen and the pines, you could almost hear, "Carry On." But all that was later, too.

Maybe the biggest name of them all who ended up in our fair state arrived in Denver third-billed to Ten Years After for a gig at a downtrodden roller rink on South Broadway in 1968. When Joe Cocker came on stage, nobody you knew had ever heard of the guy and once he started singing nobody ever forgot him. Joe just blasted the room that night and every other time you saw him, except at the Denver Pop Festival, where he confessed to being scared to death, not of performing but of the riot taking place at the gates.

There are many great stories about him, this guy who won Grammies and Academy Awards and was in many people's estimation one of the two or three truly great singers of that time from the United Kingdom (Van Morrison and Tom Jones being the others, although the mind boggles at all the rest of them who just might make a claim). Your favorite is when his very cool road manager, Peetie Knapp (one of his many names), and the famed Geitz Romo, most recently of Romo's Roadside Relics on Highway 119 as you came swooping down the canyon into Nederland and now a guide of this mighty road show supporting Joe's latest tour, gathered the band, the roadies, and the rest of the entourage for a day of fishing at a high mountain lake in the Rockies, maybe Red Feather or another near by.

It was one of those perfect Alpine days, warm and sunny, a soft breeze stirring the aspens, and everybody was digging it. Everybody that is except Joe, who was tired. He gathered himself into a fetal position on the ground beneath a tree, placed his jacket under his head, and fell fast asleep.

Everybody else was fishing and drinking beer. They would take long swigs from bottles of maybe Corona or some such and make long casts with spinning gear into that perfect lake high in the Rocky Mountains, and for more than a couple of hours, that was the scene and it was perfect except for the fact that not a single one of them caught a fish. Not even a nibble. Not one.

The bloom was coming off the rose when Joe finally stirred. The sun and the beer and the failure to communicate successfully with the trout had brought on a bit of an attitude among the fishers, who by now had concluded nice day or not that there simply weren't any fish in this lake to be had.

They explained it in great detail to Joe as he rose and wiped the sleep from his eyes and listened until he could stand it no more. He grabbed a fishing pole from one of the guys, rooted around in his greasy pair of green velvet pants, came up with his room key from the hotel in those days when keys still were made of metal, tied it carefully just above a treble hook, tossed it a long way into the lake just as the sun was setting, and reeling it in, he caught a three pound rainbow trout.

©Dan Fong 2018

Some people, you've come to learn in your time, just have the magic and Joe Cocker was one of them. He became famous at Woodstock, played venues large and small for more than 30 years, filled them all and sold more records than anyone could imagine, and one day purchased Mad Dog Ranch in Crawford, Colorado, where he built a mansion in the woods at the foot of mighty peaks and which he and his wife called home for many years until his death in 2014.

Maybe you were visiting friends in Hotchkiss or Paonia one afternoon and the serene sunset was briefly disturbed by the beating rotor of a helicopter flying in from the airport in Grand Junction an hour's drive away. And everybody in your party paused for just a minute to cock their heads toward the sound, listened a moment, took it in and one of them said, "Joe's back," and the others nodded, "Yep, he is."

A Denver kid named Mick Manressa and a kid from Yonkers, New York named Harold Fielden built a band unlike any other. Flash Cadillac and the Continental Kids was retro before retro was hip, before, in fact, most of us even knew there was anything to be retro about. With their greased back hair and their Fifties outfits, they played ferocious rock & roll while they cranked out a stage show second to none. They rocked Tulagi's and every other club in Boulder where they played, and when you wandered in one night to catch their act, it stressed your studied nonchalance that the twist contest they incited from the stage progressed very quickly to dancers all over the room who were naked ("Skin to Win"). American Graffiti is just an afterthought in your recollection of them, but a good one.

Latter day Flash Cadillac c. 1978
credit: Carnegie Library for Local History/Boulder Daily Camera Collection

Unknown musicians of great talent began arriving from everywhere. A guy named Brad Miller from who knows where had a band called Sky King and at his invitation, you went one night to catch a rehearsal, jamming in the basement of a building in the heart of Denver. In those days, the office buildings and stores downtown emptied out at 5 p.m. and everyone went home. Everyone except the homeless, the bums, the street people, and a whole lot of freaks who were making room for themselves in those beautiful brick buildings that still remained after the Skyline Urban Renewal Project had leveled most of downtown and put up all those antiseptic skyscrapers.

You're walking through the streets around Arapahoe or Curtis, the night soft and warm, down the alley to where Sky King is rehearsing and you hear a sound unlike anything that band has ever made. When you get there, a kid with long black hair streaked with ribbons of color is playing the most outrageous guitar you've ever heard. "Name is Tommy Bolin," Brad tells you. "He's like 16 or something. Just got here from Iowa or Ohio or some damn place. Pretty fuckin' awesome player."

Tommy and a guy named Jeff Cook had a band called American Standard that played some screaming rock & roll. They met a couple of kids from Brown Sugar, David and Candy Givens, who were new to Boulder, just in from Aspen. John Faris and Robbie Chamberlin joined them, Jeff got dumped, and Zephyr was born.

The band never really came together as we all kept expecting. The players were plenty talented, and by any standards Candy and Tommy were among the very best anywhere at what they did. But it never quite jelled.

Maybe they were done in by ego, a not unusual failing in the business. Maybe it was mismanagement, because theirs always struck you as sketchy. Um, ABC was their label, right? Who knew they sold records? They sure as hell didn't sell many. Who made that deal, anyhow?

You knew them and loved them and wanted to see them reach the vast potential everybody saw. They were Boulder's band for a few years in the way that the Astronauts had been a few light years before. Many great players and a lot of very good bands were working, but Zephyr was the one we thought was perfect for the time and would do it in a big way. They never did.

As David Givens has described it, Tommy eventually went over to the dark side, chasing stardom by replacing Joe Walsh in the James Gang and, later on, playing lead for Deep Purple. He also played with people like Herbie Hancock, Jimi Hendrix, and many others of that magnitude in his tragically brief career. A few solo albums, some session work, and a lot of indelible impressions he made on audiences everywhere he played have sustained his reputation as one of the very great musicians ever to pass our way. A guitar god. One of the few things he failed to achieve was the "27 club." He died at 25.

Candy lasted a little longer. She died in 1984 at age 37. Of all the women who came to the stage in that testosterone-dominated time, she was among the very best singers, period. Candy Ramey Givens was a Colorado girl and a singer without peer in a very tough business that was not geared to women. She held her own wherever she played and thrilled everyone who ever heard her. You saw so many gigs of hers and never were less than astonished by her talent. Sadly, in her too brief time with us, she never got the acclaim she was due.

ZEPHYR

One of the most amazing of all those players who came to town was Tim Duffy, who arrived in Boulder from New England, formed Orchestra of Clouds, a sort of freeflowing, amorphous group of musicians who came and went in various combinations, playing indefinable music of a kind that people today still talk about and still can't label accurately. Funk and blues, jazz and acid rock, and various extemporaneous riffs that no one had heard before. There's a well-known story from the days when Tim and Reed McRoberts and all those other folks would gather to rehearse. Duffy would draw weird shapes on pieces of paper, hold them up and say, "Play that!" Which was pretty much the way it sounded.

A screaming redhead with a big voice and a personality to match showed up in town around this time. Lannie Garrett got her first local gig with Ron Henry and Pride, where you got to know her, and then with one band and another over the next 5 decades, quickly becoming Denver's favorite chanteuse. When you caught her Patsy DeCline act and noticed the huge following she had in the gay community, you thought of Bette Midler's club scene in New York. But Lannie was absolutely herself and like no other, in this town or elsewhere. Not many have lasted so long so well.

People like Chris Daniels blew into town from Minnesota around 1971, joined the famed jam band, Magic Music, and stuck around through various iterations like his longest-lived band, the Kings, came to run Swallow Hill Music for many years and even one day would become director of the Colorado Music Hall of Fame when that place finally decided it was way past

Dusty Drapes & The Dusters

due for an upgrade. But that was far off in the future. For now, he and Magic Music were just part of a beautiful, phenomenal and unprecedented scene that was blooming like wildflowers in the meadows.

Steve Swenson was another Minnesotan who arrived in Colorado around 1970 and ended up in Evergreen rooming with Don DeBacker, the bad ass guitarist from 60,000,000 Buffalo who was gigging here and there with Dan McCorison. The three of them, Rick Schmidt, and Tommy Evans became the first iteration of Dusty Drapes and the Dusters, one of the seminal country rock bands that maybe presaged Commander Cody and Asleep at The Wheel in defining that genre. Whatever the truth of that, Dusty and the boys were one of the best dance bands in town. They really packed them in, and bars like Peggy's Hi-Lo out on 30th at the Longmont Diagonal never would have been what they were without them. Maybe vice versa, too.

You used to live in an old farmhouse just across the Diagonal from the Hi-Lo, close enough in fact that on a summer night with the windows open you could hear Dusty and the boys wailing away. More than once, you beat feet up the driveway, through the little church cemetery across the road, sprinted like a mad man across the highway, and took in a few beers and a few tunes from the bar. It was rare that there wasn't a full house. You were glad to fit in.

You and Mike Jacobson had an art gallery at 1909 Broadway. A lot of people hung out there, including a lot of these musicians. It was one of the stops on the circuit as you made your way through the day. You met a lot of talent there.

Stanley Sheldon would come to Boulder from Ottawa, Kansas, Jock Bartley from Hutchison, Max Grunenthal from next door in the little town of Humphrey, Nebraska, and more like them just kept coming.

Stanley was an incredible talent, one of those people when you got to know him who made you realize his hands worked differently than yours. When he gripped a bass guitar and his fingers began moving rhythmically up and down the neck, pinching each string at precisely the fret that squeezed out sublime sounds in perfect time, you came to realize that this talent he had was of a different order than anything musically you might ever bring to the table.

After his time with Tommy Bolin and Energy, Stanley gigged here and there all over town with one band and another. Like most musicians, he loved to play and made just enough money to survive from one day to the next.

One inauspicious day, when he got kicked out of Shannon's, which was somewhere near the very end of the road in Boulder, although it was conveniently located right downtown, and where he'd been playing for peanuts, he came by your gallery to see Jake the Snake and ask to borrow a little coin. "Screw it," he said, "I'm going to L.A. to seek my fortune." Six months later, he was playing bass in the Oakland Coliseum in front of 100,000 fans in preparation for Peter Frampton Comes Alive, for 30 years or more the biggest selling live, double album in history.

Max was a visitor to the gallery almost daily, taking a bit of a break from his relentless routine of practicing scales on the piano and singing scales in different keys, all day, every day, while his beautiful, somewhat shy spouse taught school to put bread on the table. The day would come when, under the name Max Carl, he would sing lead for Jack Mack and the Heart Attack, and then for .38 Special, and has since sung lead for Grand Funk Railroad, among other big name bands.

Jock sold guitars and miscellaneous stuff for Nick the Greek at his big music shop on 17th and Pearl, played with Candy and David and John Faris and Otis Taylor in Etheral Zephyr after Tommy Bolin left for the James Gang, and hung around your gallery looking for the big opportunity or really any opportunity at all, which came one night in Nederland at the Pioneer Inn when he was playing the opening set at a gig headlining Gram Parsons and Emmylou Harris.

Jock in those days was pretty shy and played from the shadows of the stage, almost with his back to the audience. Gram was doing coke in his trailer out back, or maybe something stronger, when the sweetest guitar sounds he'd ever heard reached his ringing ears. He and Emmylou stumbled into the bar in time to hear Jock taking a solo that simply blew them away. A couple of days later, Jock was nicely suited up by Nudie in the finest western piping to play lead with Gram Parsons, Emmylou Harris & the Fallen Angels. A few years later, he would join up with Rick Roberts, who had replaced Parsons in the Flying Burrito Brothers, to form Firefall. By then, he wasn't shy anymore.

The migration worked both directions. Maurice White hired a young kid from East High by the name of Philip Bailey to sing his stunning falsetto lead vocals for Earth, Wind & Fire. He was joined later by fellow Angels Larry Dunn and Andrew Woolfolk in what was one of the most successful groups of the 70s.

Not all of the musicians who came to town in those days would find fame and fortune, but their presence in Colorado, the bands they eventually came to play with, and the music scene they helped to grow was part of what attracted even more talent to the state. Like those who came here, a lot of the folks who were already here, and those like Bailey and Jello Biafra, who left Colorado for L.A., where he founded the Dead Kennedys, they eventually played the big stage and brought some of their band mates back to Colorado with them.

One of the hottest and longest lived bands came to town from Arizona after paying some serious dues in L.A. The Freddi-Henchi Band was like no other in Colorado, laying down a soulful, funky sound while putting on a full-blown R&B show—flashy costumes, dance routines, and all. Freddie Gowdy and Marvin Graves led the party band of the Seventies, a show that was more an East Coast/Midwest soul review than the acid rock scene they entered.

Their agent booked them at Sam's or the Green Onion or somewhere in Fort Collins and they arrived "in our California clothes," Fred Gowdy recalled. "We were freezing." But they must have liked what they saw because soon enough they'd relocated to Colorado. For a while, they were more or less the house band at the Good Earth in Boulder out on 28th, but it seemed to you at one time or another you caught them at nearly every club in Denver, too: the Piccadilly, Basins Up, Skunk Creek Inn, the Shapes, among lots of others, and they always filled the house.

When people talk about "soul" music, or "R&B," or "funk," they're talking about black music, regardless of the color of the players. It's a sound that Freddi-Henchi brought to town. Not that other people couldn't play it, just that these guys did it better than anybody else.

Freddi-Henchi and the Soulsetters, Boulder, CO 1970

Gowdy was walking past Tulagi's one day and saw on the marquee: The Average White Band. Cool name, he thought, and came back that night to catch their act. There were about 8 people in the audience.

He introduced himself, told them he liked their name and now that he'd heard it, he liked their music, too. You should come by the Good Earth tonight when you're done here and jam with us, he told them. They did for four nights straight and the two bands came together seamlessly. They were awesome, the crowd loved it, the Tule was still nearly empty for their gigs, but they got some serious exposure playing with the Freddi-Henchi Band. A year later, the Average White Band was all over the charts, having some major success. Freddie-Henchi was still reliably tearing 'em up in town.

Nobody else in Colorado was playing their kind of music and they never lacked for gigs or an audience that was ready to party with them. They flat out cooked, and nobody but nobody could sit through one of their tunes. If you saw somebody seated while the band was doing, "I Just Want to Dance, Dance," chances were good that person was dead, whether or not they knew it.

Where did the rest of them come from? Fly McClard played with just about everybody that was anybody for most of the Seventies, beginning with Fly and the Zippers all the way to playing horns with Dusty Drapes and the Dusters. There weren't a lot of horns in rock bands at the time, Bobby Keys being the big-time exception, but Fly was welcomed everywhere and made many a band rework their lineup to make room for him.

A classic example of the way bands in those days came and went was The Legendary 4nikators, who had at least two thundering iterations in the Seventies alone, and uncounted, maybe uncountable, variations ever since. Harold Fielden was back in town after parting from Flash Cadillac. He wanted

Gerry Jimmerfield from Durango, Colorado

to form another hard-charging rock and roll performance band and he asked the folks in Zephyr. They and a rhythm guitarist named Dave Brown came together every so often in alternative mode, dressed in weird costumes and playing covers of a lot of hot tunes by the name bands of the era.

After a while, Harold went to grad school, Zephyr was touring and the 4nikators dissolved. A couple of years later, maybe '72 or '73, after Zephyr went south, Energy went south, and both bands left a lot of burned out players in their wake, Harold like a phoenix returned to the scene, this time with his old sidekick, Mick Manressa from Flash, Mac Ferris from Fuchs, Otis Taylor from many gigs with many different bands, and Tommy Bolin, Candy and David Givens from the original band. They were incandescent, and when you saw them a couple of times at Art's Bar & Grill, packing them in and rocking hard, you thought to yourself it had been a long time since you saw David, Candy and Tommy having so much fun. Unfortunately, it was not to last, but it was very good while it did.

Musicians were arriving from far and wide, and some from not so far away, like Michael Woody from Yuma and Gerry Jimmerfield from Durango. Gerry's band was known at various times in various guises as The Lords of London and maybe even Dragonfly, but for those of us who knew them best and loved them most, they could only be The Jimmerfield Legend. They played bars all over the Western Slope and clubs up and down the front range, and even ventured to L.A. a time or two, bringing their very hot

Too High Band

and slightly twisted boogie-woogie (called for the Doctor and the Doctor said...) even to the Family Dog, when it was in its brief, red-hot glory.

In 1968, Woody was in Boulder at C.U. with Jock Bartley, Harold Fielden and Chris Lowe of Flash Cadillac, Fly McClard and who knows who all among the many musicians haunting the dormitories and dreaming their dreams. His band, Woody and the Peckers, played every bar in town repeatedly, had a huge following among folks who liked to dance, and came to be The Too High Band as years went by and the boozy nights accumulated.

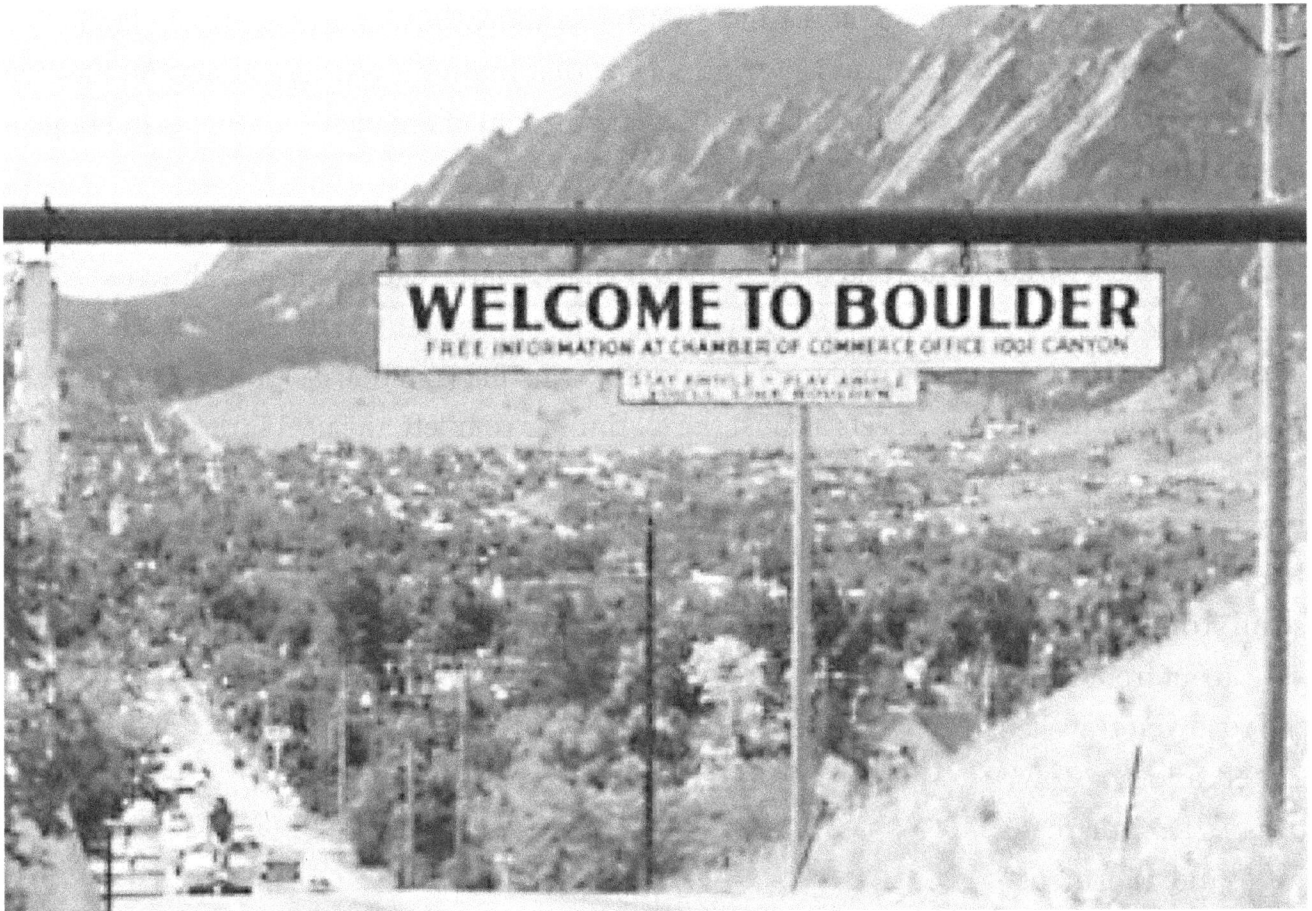

11

HIGHER

SOMETIMES IT SEEMED TO YOU BOULDER was a warp in the space-time continuum and that for complicated cosmic reasons beyond your comprehension, everybody sooner or later wanted to be there. It was like a doorway, a gateway, an entry point. Once you passed those portals, something in you changed and you never left. Not for long. You might go away. The tour might be calling, big bucks await, the chance of a lifetime, again and again. But you always came back. Like paradise. Like a rut. You can never truly leave. You've been gone from there since 1979 and you still can feel it in your heart. That was true of so many people from so many different walks of life. It was true of musicians, too.

The pervasive inclination of those times was to rise above the mania of the urban landscape and "get away." If you were from New York or for that matter anywhere along the Eastern corridor, Colorado was something like the hidden kingdom of Shangri-La. Om, as in home, it seemed to be.

If you came to town from Rocky Mountain National Park, down along either branch of the river from Estes Park to Lyons and then south to Boulder, a large wrought iron arch across North Broadway welcomed you to town. But rather, if like most everyone, you first saw Boulder as you crested the last long rise on the road from Denver, it was an image you'd never forget. The Flatirons rose up in tall, sheer granite sheets against the foothills to your left, the neat little town gathered in a brilliant green bowl at the foot of the mountains, the sandstone campus spread out from where the road you travelled ended and the town began, the little roads here and there rose up the canyons to the snow shrouded Continental Divide, and mighty Longs Peak loomed to your right. As in high!

The concept of getting high meant different things to different people at different times, but the essence was transcendence. You wanted to get above it all and nowhere in the USA was higher than Colorado. Denver was the Mile High City, the Queen City of the Plains, and Boulder was your very first, smack-dab encounter with the place where the mountains rose up from them and lifted you into the sky.

Perhaps, then, it was no accident that a sort of local boy with a too wholesome manner and an altogether too commercial sound for the times nevertheless sold more records than any other single artist based in Colorado.

His name was John Denver and his signature song was "Rocky Mountain High." Corny or not, it spoke to exactly the concept that brought so many people, musicians among them, to the exalted alpine empire of Colorado.

So, too, at nearly the same time, "Rocky Mountain Way" (couldn't get much higher), which Joe Walsh and Kenny Passarelli wrote about the joy they and Barnstorm felt in getting back to Colorado after time on the road, spoke to that same consciousness. Just as Jimmy Guercio was constructing his studio at Caribou Ranch outside Nederland, the place where even John Lennon recorded, Elton John cut three albums, and Michael Jackson nearly took up residence, the siren song of Colorado was being broadcast far and wide.

The thing about Denver and a few other places in Colorado was that people throughout the Midwest always had gathered here, looking for something different than the farms, the fields of wheat and corn, the suffocating strictures of small town life, the dominance of religion and the paucity of culture. Part of the state's attraction was its ski industry, of course, which brought a lot of people here to hit the slopes, stop at some point on their trip to stare at the sky and the peaks and the snow and say to themselves, "Wow! This is pretty fine," and go back home telling tales of the Rockies.

Dan Fogelberg talked about driving through the Rockies in maybe 1971 or '72 and saying to himself, "If I ever make some money, this is where I'm gonna live." Dan was from Illinois and like a lot of other flatlanders passing through, he was taken by the sheer beauty of the place. A few year later, he announced from the stage at Ebbets Field that he was buying a house in Nederland the next day, which became his home until well into the '80s and his inspiration for Nether Lands, the album he wrote during his first year there.

You remember Linda Wearley talking about her first trip from Ohio to San Francisco back then. She passed through Colorado on the way and happened to camp out near the Maroon Bells her first night here. "I'd heard of stars," she said of that experience, "but I'd never seen them before."

Most everywhere else was flat, but Colorado was three dimensional. It had the slopes, it had wide open spaces, and it had a pretty cool city in Denver. And a pretty cool town in Boulder. And Aspen. And a lot of little nooks and crannies throughout the state that seemed to be the locus of "high." Between Chicago and San Francisco, there was Denver. As a city, maybe it wasn't much in comparison to New York or Los Angeles, but it was way more than nearly anywhere else out here and, literally, loftier than any of them by a mile.

————

Maybe you remember some things that struck you from out of the blue about what was happening, even if you didn't quite grasp it at the time. A wink of the future in the corner of your eye. Once was when, in a quintessentially colonial enclave of Connecticut, you were a very young man first venturing far afield, a dyed-in-the-wool Yankee named Jim Zarbock, whose daughter, Heidi, you were courting, looked at you askance and said, "You're from Colorado? Whatever reason could you possibly have for wanting to live here? Everybody here wants to be there!"

Another was a few years later in a checkout line at the Liquor Mart in Boulder, where you and all your friends spent a fair amount of coin on lubrication, when you happened to notice a rack of Readers Digest magazines with a banner across the front of them proclaiming, "Colorado, the Closest Place to Heaven." Something in you sifted thoughts of "ten million people read that rag" and "our little town and our little state may never be the same again." And then you took your six pack of cold brews or your bottle of a good red wine home and thought not a lot about it again until it happened right before your eyes.

Until it did, though, until Boulder morphed over the years into the world's largest shopping center; until Denver became a sea of high-priced condominiums washed up against the foothills; until the Front Range became one continuous metropolitan area from Cheyenne to Pueblo; until then, when the Sixties were just turning to the Seventies and everybody still had stars in their eyes, it was a remarkable place to be.

12

PERCEPTION

THE BURST OF CREATIVITY that attended those days wasn't limited to music. Not even to the arts. People in every imaginable endeavor were exploring new ways to do what they do. In business as in leisure, in art and culture, in spiritual pursuits and debauchery, in every manner of living and how we conducted our lives, the grand experiment was underway.

And what a cast of characters. Since 1965, Drop City outside Trinidad, Colorado had housed a collection of artists and miscellaneous bohemians in geodesic domes constructed of sheet metal

from wrecked cars. Clark Richert, who later would chair the art department at Rocky Mountain College and become one of the state's very finest painters, founded the commune with fellow artists, Richard Kallweit, and JoAnn and Gene Bernofsky. Based on their concept of Drop Art, honed as students at the University of Kansas, it was an experiment in artistic innovation that within a few years had attracted people from all over the world to join in the fun.

In 1967, they hosted the Joy Festival, won a Dymaxion award from Bucky Fuller for their domes, and became noted nationally when the Firesign Theatre included them in a tongue-in-cheek commercial ("Send the top of your dad's car to Drop City, Colorado").

As communes went, they never had the cachet of the Hog Farm in New Mexico, and Clark wasn't media-ready as Wavy Gravy, but Drop City was a phenomenon very early in the game. They lasted until the late Seventies and many of them then beat feet to Boulder.

There were artists of the movement already settled in Boulder by then, people like Dianne Stromberg, who created images in those very early days like the famed Boulder t-shirt, the furbearing trout, and Slumber Party in Santa Fe, art that spoke to the times so clearly and cleanly, you always loved her and her work. Over the years, she has put so many beautiful images and so much food for thought in your humble brainpan, you can only thank her for continuing to drop by and be a part of your life.

Then, too, the day in August of 1972 when you rounded a curve on the highway near Rifle on the way back to Boulder and saw stretched between the sides of the gap the Valley Curtain, Christo's 200,000 square foot sunburst orange drape built by one Theodore Dougherty's A and H Builders of Boulder — that was hallucinatory! You would come to know Christo and Jeanne-Claude in later years but for now it was just another stunning encounter with monumental creativity.

Some of the really notable artists of the time labored in relative obscurity, creating concert posters for Chet Helms and Bill Graham at $25 apiece that were nailed to telephone poles and taped to windows all over San Francisco and, because of the Family Dog when it came to town, in every nook and cranny of the Front Range for a very short period of time. Rick Griffin, Victor Moscoso, Stanley Mouse, Alton Kelley, Bob Schnepf, and Wes Wilson, each of them was an innovator and each a purveyor of what commonly came to be called Psychedelic Art, a style of illustration that had something in common with Impressionism, something in common with Expressionism, and a lot in common with LSD, it is assumed.

This wasn't done with desktop publishing; rather, these incredibly intricate and detailed designs were executed with a separate rubylith or amberlith masking film cutout for each color. And there was a lot of color. These guys originated a style of illustration that still is unique to them 50 years later.

They, and people like the extraordinary Gilbert Shelton, creator of the Furry Freak Brothers, and R. Crumb, creator of Mr. Natural and Fritz the Cat, who birthed an entire cast of cartoon characters that were a perfect personification of the people of that time, warts and all, were the true artists of that brief, clear window of perception. Crumb in his brief time in Boulder was persuaded by Marcello Cabus, Jr. to execute a series of plywood cutouts of the artist's famous characters, which were used to decorate the walk in front of his store, Cotangent, for its second iteration on Pearl Street in downtown Boulder. Something like having Picasso paint you a yard sign. One wonders where they now reside and what patina they've gathered over time? They are classic images of the era.

13

THE GOOD STUFF

An entire tribe of kids from florida and other parts down South arrived en masse in town. They were known variously as the Range Riders or the Pickle Gulch Gang, the latter for their communal digs outside Rollinsville, just a few miles above Black Hawk, in the days before gambling when it was just another sleepy town, and the former for their penchant to dress like cowboys and Indians of a distinctly hippie manner. They were led by a guy named David Casey, an Air Force brat born in Japan and raised all over the world, most recently of Orlando, who was smart, charismatic, and deeply committed to his family. He greeted you every time with the peace sign, a beautiful smile and a twinkle in his eye that said to you, "It's all cool." In retrospect, he still seems to you to perfectly epitomize the times you shared and the ways that things played out.

The Range Riders came to town in buckskin garb and serapes, beaded vests and pipe bags originally worn by Plains tribes of Native Americans, and all manner of sashes, embroidered stuff, battered cowboy hats, or pirate scarves, and leather knife sheaths with big blades that had seen some use. They arrived in old pickup trucks or Mercedes sedans, whatever was running that particular day, and whoever was with them, be it Bob or Michael Casey, Tommy Byrd, Greg Gable, Clean Dean or any of the other guys, it was always a remarkable scene and one you were glad to be a part of.

David turned you on to Chateau d'Yquem, which was rarefied stuff even then and priced accordingly. He was buying the '47 at $28 a bottle, which is equivalent to maybe $200 today, but considering that a bottle of that particular vintage now is worth about $15,000, it was a bargain and an astute investment. Assuming you didn't consume it first, of course.

Drawing by Little Boy of the STP Family, early '70s, Boulder

One fine day, when you and Tommy or Greg or one of the boys enjoyed a small windfall and happened to meet up at the Liquor Mart, you convinced each other that buying three magnums of the '59 was a splendid idea and you did. There was a reasonably good supply available and, timing being everything, a little cash met a desirable product and a purchase was made.

You drove up Boulder Canyon, through Nederland and Rollinsville all the way to Pickle Gulch, kicked back under a tree in a meadow on a beautiful day with a bowl or two of something or other and one entire magnum of that very fine Sauternes, and, after a while in a slightly inebriated state, had the good sense to conclude that the other two magnums needed to be hidden away for now, being an investment you wanted to preserve.

So, you got a shovel from the trunk of the car and a small canvas bag to store them in, then set about digging a hole sufficiently deep and wide to hold the cache, but not one so big as to be in any way obvious after you carefully buried the stash and skillfully masked any evidence that the ground had been disturbed. You clasped hands with your co-conspirator, bonked heads, gave each other a very big smile and went on about your day.

When you woke up the next morning in one of the fine cabins in the family compound and enjoyed a wonderful breakfast that Laurie provided us, you asked Tommy or Greg or whoever it was if they remembered where we had buried the stash. "Sure," he said and you said you thought that you did, too.

The thing about sauternes, even the best of them, is that they are meant to be consumed in moderation; otherwise, they can give you a helluva hangover. But you are young and strong and dumb, and so is he, and, so, with a bellyful of an excellent breakfast and a bit of a ferocious headache, you saddle up a couple of horses and push ahead into the day.

When you reach the meadow of the day before, everything looks familiar. Familiar and the same. There are a lot of trees and long stretches of grass with wildflowers growing everywhere. Everywhere you look, it appears a lot alike.

You stumble around from one place to another for more than an hour. It dawns on you finally you haven't a clue. In a moment that presages Fargo by a couple of decades, you look to the left and you look to the right and the fence in the snow stretches on forever. Maybe the Coen Brothers were watching.

If there is any benefit to the wholesale development of Colorado and the frantic bite of the excavators tearing up its every place of beauty as this story is being told, it is perhaps that some poorly paid, hot and sweaty heavy equipment operator will notice the rotted fabric of a canvas bag his shovel uncovers near the roots of a tree in a meadow north of Black Hawk, and taking the time to climb down from his seat, wipe his brow with a handkerchief and lift the bag from the dirt, he will find two well preserved and very valuable magnums of fine wine. The internet being what it is, a quick search will tell him he's sitting on a $5K bonus.

There were colorful characters everywhere you looked in Boulder in those days. Clancy the Leprechaun, Terry the Pirate, Little Doug, Little Benji, Sam the Smuggler Man, Chick Slick, Geitz Romo (How to Talk Hip) and Candy, Junior and Rosie, Marty and Lucy, Sandy and Mary Rose, Butch and Mary, Demetrius and Shelia, Laurie Long and everybody, you and

Becky, Linda and others, Nicky Angelo, Sandra, Wyck, Beth and John Hay, Mo and Peggy, Bob Gilnick and the wonderful singer he shared a home with for several years, Michael Agitator, David Roscoe, Chaz, Hank and Charlie, Jake the Snake and Little Jake, Ricky and Zip, exquisite Pam Evans, Jimmy Cotton, Terry Toole, Yank Mojo, Valdor and Sweet Virginia, Zullo, Lonesome Lorenzo, David Chamberlain, Marcus, Randy Crazy Horse, and the rest of the boy guru crowd, the ravishing Leslie at the Walrus, Peggy Sunshine, Alan Armstrong, and Slinky Link (Rene, Rene, who got away), Pamela, Cynthia, Barbara and Greg, Blue Tantari, Peggy Jessel, tall, curly-haired Lizzy, Miss Kitty, Tim and Rachel, Russell and Sylvia, Jackie, Constance, the incredible, inevitable Tita; and, the Nordic Queen, the Four Aces, Toby and Dick at the Brillig Works, Dee, who mid-wifed Deva, and Little Mary, Felix and Ellen, Link and Lefty, Billy and Patty, Will and Yvonne, Black Mo, Blond Mo, Char, Paula, Bernard and Mary, Kristine in the chamois dress, the woman, what was her name, with the bangles and beads, Valerie, Becky Lillstrom, Terri and all those incredible seamstresses at Cotangent on the Hill, and beautiful Abby Kavanagh, and on and on. You remember so many more faces but the names...

There was the Haystack Mountain commune, and all the folks who gathered there around Steve and Babs, for whom peace and love was all; and, at the other end of that spectrum, Whiskey John and the STP family, who put it all to the test; and in between those extremes all the dogs, too. Smooth Dog, Spiffy Dog, Black Dog, Red Dog, plus all the other characters who blew through town on a regular basis from way down south, Gyro, Douglas, Joe Alito, Rubio and Humps, John, Boogie, Spoolie and the UA crowd, the boys from Brownsville, the surfers from La Jolla who had their own boat, and Ron from Peru, and all the others who always preferred to remain nameless. And, of course, all the musicians.

Sometimes, your memory connects to people from the very early days in Boulder, back when, if you can believe it, there were no traffic lights in town, just some flashing yellow lights where Broadway curved around the campus and met 13th Street before heading downtown. Everywhere else, stop signs did the job.

Some of your pals from those times are rarely and then only vaguely recalled. David Bradley, Debbie Hickox from Ohio, Stephanie from California, Peter and what was her name with her legs in the air, Alan and Kitty, Charlie Biggers, John Pepinere who loved Nancy Wilson, Liz from up near Baseline who was such a comfort, Denny the drummer missing most of his fingers who played with Mose Allison, Denise the tall, cool beauty from Wisconsin, the very rowdy Pi Phis, the sorta classy Tri-Delts, all those cold nights sleeping outdoors, the cemetery on 9th Street, the backyards along the ditch below Sewall Hall, the basements on the Hill, the roomy walk-in closet where you finally found a bed for more than a night or two, and began to settle in.

One fellow you'll never forget was the old guy in the coat and tie, food stains all over them both, who used to wander into Bennett's Pizza and order a cup of spumoni ice cream, part of which he would consume and part of which he added to the rest of the stains on his clothes as it dribbled off his chin.

For a time, you slept in the basement, among the cases of canned tomato sauce and the bags of high-gluten flour stacked in towers, past the industrial mixers where your bed was tucked in a nook under the big metal gates in the sidewalk above where footfalls of the passersby rang like iron thunder; and as a resident you felt proprietary about the place and the customers, and poor as you were, it was guys like that bumbling old man with the ice cream stains and the aimless smile who made you feel you were pretty well off after all.

Most of you felt sorry for him, he seemed so hapless, and always comped him the cup of ice cream. It was a bit of a shock when you learned that Ol' Spumoni, as he had come to be called, actually owned the building where you lived and worked and about half the others on the Hill. That was Boulder in the day. So many good people and so many great memories.

The author, Scotty Coen, Mick Hirsch, early '70s, Denver

14

TURN IT UP

A YOUNG HIPSTER CHARACTER by the name of Steve Thoresen in 1969 sweet-talked Robert Neil Wilkinson into accessing his radio station in Boulder. KRNW-FM was a one man operation, the one man being Bob, who literally had built the station in a closet in his home and gradually over the years, playing four hours of classical music from 6 to 10 p.m. each evening, had graduated to a very funky studio on the second floor of a dive building on Pearl Street east of 13th Street.

The studio had one turntable and a monaural signal (so he said, although we eventually learned otherwise), a library consisting of a few dozen symphony orchestra recordings, and a potential that nobody, not Bob, or Steve, or any of a few dozen freaks who came to spin tunes there, had a inkling of what it was someday to become. In the not too distant future, it would be mighty KBCO-FM, with a big time 50,000 watt transmitter and an audience up and down the Front Range that killed the ratings and was valued in the tens of millions of dollars. But, for now, it was local radio and thanks to Steve, the freaks got their hands on it and made it happen.

He and you alternated nights to begin with, following the classical show with free-form rock & roll from 10 p.m. 'til 2 a.m. Headhunter and The Electric Cowboy, you called yourselves, and had a great time playing tunes that nobody else was playing and everybody wanted to hear. You had a ton of albums from your gig reviewing music for the local rag, and the audience locally if small in numbers was absolutely huge in appetite and appreciation.

People would stroll into the studio from off the streets with big spliffs and bottles of wine, six packs, presents of all sorts, and very good looking friends of every persuasion. There was the ever present, industrial sized dispenser of Ozium at the ready, so when the door at the bottom of the stairs opened, and unidentified parties began to climb them, a squirt or two in one direction and another cleared the air of anything lingering there. Until everyone got comfortable again and another doobie flared.

You'd play a raucous cut from one album, maybe the Doors doing Strange Days, and when it hit the final bars, you'd rip it off the turntable, plop down Are You Experienced, hope to hit the exact groove to start Purple Haze, and let Jimi blow them away. New material was being released nearly every week, great tunes by favorite players or newly formed bands you'd never heard before who quickly became favorites.

There was almost nowhere else that people could hear this music on the radio, other than maybe a cut from some of these albums that would pop up like clockwork, same time, same station, every day, on the formatted FM stations. It was such a pleasure and an education for announcer and listener alike to roam through these albums, one after another, and play whatever felt right to you at the moment. You developed an intense loyalty to your audience and they to you.

Some nights you'd be there all alone, and maybe a melodious voice would call you on the phone, saying "Please play 'River Deep, Mountain High' for me," and you'd say, "Okay," and she'd say, "I'll be right down." And even before Ike and Tina killed those final bars, in walked all six feet of Andi Wiardi, who was blonde and brazen and luminous, so gorgeous she was absolutely breathtaking, and you knew at that moment, all things considered, that life was simply fine.

Boulder was a small, tight knit community in those days. Little by little the KRNW audience grew and more hours were added to the broadcast day. Bob became more and more concerned about what exactly this creature was that he had wrought, but the die decidedly was cast, the monster was beginning to twitch and soon it would be standing. Maybe walking, even.

Brian Kreizenbeck, the very first free-form radio guy in Colorado, freshly back from Massachusetts, where he did a gig at WMAS-FM after being run out of Denver radio for general creativity, was the first hire. Bob had his doubts about him, baggage and all that, but Steve was convincing and the infamous Super Warthog joined the lineup. Next was Bill Ashford, who literally grew up in radio on the East Coast and migrated West over time. They were joined by Sandy Phelps, a folk singer by trade and one of the very few women in the radio business in those days when, notoriously, rock was cock. Sandy had done the Village in the day, was friends with Carolyn Hester, got tight eventually with Katy Moffat, Judy Roderick, lots of the players and especially the women tough enough to make it in that male-oriented business. She was nobody's fool. Bob wanted a female on the air, expecting she'd give helpful hints and cooking tips for housewives. Fat chance! Maybe hints on 12 bar blues and contrapuntal rhythms. She knew the music and rolled out exceptional sets on the air, day after day. Nobody was better.

Brian and Bill bailed before long, headed off to KMPX in San Francisco. Mick Hirsch, aka Buffalo Chip, was one replacement of several new hires, his brother, Reno Nevada, may have been another, maybe not, and finally, KRNW was rocking 20 hours a day, while the entrenched classical show continued to anchor the 6 – 10 p.m. slot. There was minimal advertising from local merchants who were tossing a few dollars into the till, marijuana dealers mostly were paying the meager salaries, and everybody was rocking.

There was a time in Boulder in those days when you could walk down any street in town, flashing peace signs at your friends and people you didn't yet know, and go on about your business from one place to another, and you'd never miss a tune that was playing. Because, in those days after transistor radios and way before boom boxes, you could hear the music pouring out the open windows and doorways of nearly every home and business in town. "Turn it up," said Van Morrison, "little bit higher, so you'll know, radio." You did just that. KRNW was truly community radio, like the pulse of a small town with a whole lot of heart.

©Dan Fong 2018

The Who at Mammoth Gardens, Denver 1970

15

HEAT AND HOW IT WORKS

IF THE FIRST WAVE OF THIS STORY began with Harry Tuft, the second in many ways began with Barry Fey. He came to Denver from Chicago, where he had made a few tentative forays into the rock & roll trade, to promote a couple of shows for a Denver University fraternity. Before long, he was in the middle of everything of any consequence that happened in the concert business for many years to come. He was instrumental in making it a very big business, one that got big enough eventually to push him aside and, finally, to push him out.

His story has been told, often and thoroughly. If you want it direct from the horse's mouth, get Back Stage Past, his autobiography that covers the career of the man "who produced more shows, and more critically important shows, than any other concert promoter in the business." Caveat emptor, but it's pretty good stuff. Fey did a tour of his own, one final lap around the local track with Dan Fong at his side, telling one fabulous story after another, many of which were true, in promoting the book shortly before his death at 73 in 2013.

Maybe you met him when he was a normal-sized person, new in town. Before he got very big, figuratively and professionally. He was very much in the times, deeply and effectively, but not of the times like the rest of you were. He knew the people, worked with them, entertained and made money off them, but like many of the musicians he brought you, you eventually came to understand, he wasn't part of the

Postcards from the Edge / credit: The Family Dog

tribe. Where everyone else was falling all over each other in a ritual lovefest, he kept his distance, just a little, just enough. We had dreams. He had focus.

Out of nowhere, at 1601 West Evans, where the Posh had been, a new club appeared. It was called the Family Dog. Fey cut a deal with Chet Helms of the Avalon Ballroom in San Francisco to bring that music to Denver. Why that unlikely alliance was formed has been the subject of speculation: Helms was broke, it was hoped this was a step to franchising Family Dog Productions, maybe Barry Fey was just exceptionally persuasive. Whatever the reason, it was a done deal. Fey was booking the shows for the Dog. Helms was handfeeding them to him. Wow! What music it was. Denver had never seen anything like it.

On the 8th and 9th of September in 1967, Janis Joplin with Big Brother and the Holding Company headlined a show with Blue Cheer and Eighth Penny Matter. Maybe you joined Fey that first day for the sound check and when you left the room each of you mentioned with some amount of pain that Blue Cheer was so loud you could feel your thigh bones vibrating.

People turned out in droves. Fey brought one band after another to town, paired them with local groups, and put Denver in the thick of the music scene in a way it never had been before. The Dog was absolutely happening.

In less than one full year, nearly everybody who mattered in American rock & roll played there. Quicksilver Messenger Service, The Grateful Dead, Captain Beefheart, the Doors, Buffalo Springfield, Canned Heat, Allmen Joy, Sons of Champlin, The Jefferson Airplane, Jimi Hendrix, The Fugs, The Byrds, The Siegal Schwall Band, and Frank Zappa and the Mothers of Invention. Local bands like American Standard, Lothar and the Hand People, Leopold Fuchs H. Bomb, and the Jimmerfield Legend were booked there too, along with a couple of big time bands from overseas like Cream and Van Morrison. Amorphous light shows by Marc Arno of Diogenes Lantern Works, with the famous John Chick close at hand. Sound by Lee Brenk (maybe that was his name, memory fails here). Iconic posters by Bob Schnepf and the San Francisco crew of Stanley Mouse, Victor Moscoso, and the gang. Good vibes by acclaim.

About halfway through that run, Fey got the urge to start promoting shows rather than just booking them. Helms was sending the San Francisco bands, but Fey had access to L.A., where Frank Zappa and the Doors were coming on. Fey went to Harry Tuft and asked if they could co-produce Zappa and the Mothers of Invention, which Tuft agreed to do.

Harry recalls picking Zappa up at Stapleton Airport, expecting some sort of wild man and getting instead a gentleman, bright, engaging, talented, very serious about his work. He rehearsed his band that afternoon for an hour and a half, and even came into the office at the Dog before the show to count the tickets so he could verify the night's receipts.

In those uncertain times for an erratic business, you couldn't have made a better choice of a band to work with than the one Frank Zappa ran. Fey wanted Tuft with him his first time out to spread the risk if it went wrong. It all worked out. Harry remembers the profits that night as $350, split down the middle.

Fey later promoted shows at the Dog by the Doors, Cream, and several other bands who were outside Chet Helms' domain but very much a part of what was happening. Once he got started, there was no stopping him. Over the next 20 years, Fey would bring virtually every big name band in the business to Denver and several other cities he worked, as well. But that was just beginning. For the Family Dog, things were quickly coming to the end.

The Dog lasted less than a year because they fought the law and, yep, the law won. Local narcs John Gray and Jim Laurita made it their personal mission to make life miserable for as many of the kids in the audience as possible. They harassed the club's patrons relentlessly. They would line them up inside the club and search them, probable cause being that they just didn't like your looks. Cars were ticketed and towed away while kids were inside dancing. When they left after the concerts, they were frisked and often enough ("found a joint!") arrested. The culture wars had a venue now where efforts to curb the "lawlessness" could zero in on the bad guys. And focused they were.

Even the bands were victimized, rousted at their motels, searched and shaken down, and in the case of Canned Heat, reportedly according to Gray because a snitch said so, and according to the band because pot was planted on them, they were arrested, which gave birth to the band's seminal tune, "My Crime (Police in Denver Don't Want No Long Hairs Hangin' Round)."

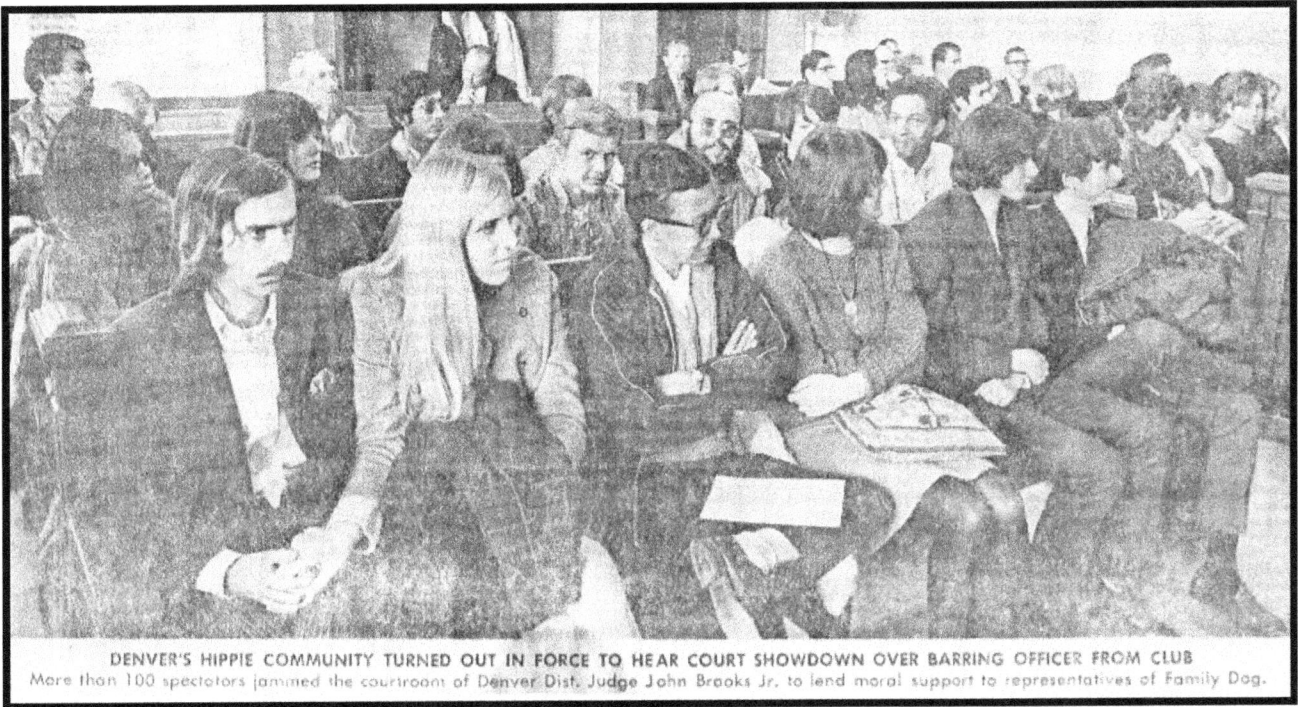

DENVER'S HIPPIE COMMUNITY TURNED OUT IN FORCE TO HEAR COURT SHOWDOWN OVER BARRING OFFICER FROM CLUB
More than 100 spectators jammed the courtroom of Denver Dist. Judge John Brooks Jr. to lend moral support to representatives of Family Dog.

Tony Guillory, Leslie Haseman, Brian Kreizenbeck and Lani Fisher (top-bottom left) credit: kfml.org

Francis Salazar, who fancied himself a high powered lawyer, owned the building where the Dog was housed. He and fellow attorney Bob Pitler worked with Fey, manager Tony Guillory, and the rest of the Dog hierarchy to enjoin the Denver Police Department from its campaign of harassment, which cooled things out for a very brief while. But it was not to be. Not for long. The brief, brilliant, glorious moment that was the Family Dog was coming to an end and Salazar himself later would have troubles of his own with the powers that be.

The Dog closed in June of 1968 appropriately with a screaming good show by Janis Joplin, who opened the club less a year before. Maybe the two of you and a few other folks drank Southern Comfort straight from the bottle that night until the floor swayed beneath you and the extraordinary beauty she was inside emerged before your eyes. Neither of you knew it was the last rock & roll show that old building would host, nor that decades of apparently more socially acceptable nude dancing would replace it in that venerable old building on West Evans. PT's has been grinding out the bucks in a haze of g-strings and cigarette smoke ever since. Rock & roll had to undergo a metamorphosis to survive.

Barry Fey learned his lessons from that experience. Going forward, he bought the law and they both won. Denver's finest, under the steady guidance of Captain Jerry Kennedy, were retained to provide security for Fey's concerts and from then on everybody pretty much went home happy.

Moonlighting was always a big part of a cop's yearly take home pay. Kennedy ran a tight ship and for many years he was arguably the most powerful cop in Colorado. When Fey got on board, rock & roll concerts became part of the entertainment infrastructure, pumping dollars into the city's tax coffers and the pockets of the favored policemen, who measurably turned down the heat. The shows were a very soft gig for the cops, good pay, little danger, cute girls, a lot of action. The kids still got harassed, but with a much lighter hand.

A contrast was Mammoth Gardens, where Stuart Green blew into town from New Jersey, bought the tired old roller rink on Colfax and Clarkson, did a modest amount of rehab, and got ready to open a club. He had big visions of competing with Bill Graham's Fillmore in San Francisco and had the good sense to come to terms with Barry Fey, who did most of the booking. But he thought he could keep the cops out. It was his club, after all.

Mammoth Gardens was an incredible dump, dirty, stuffy, insufferably hot when the room was full, with dressing rooms that looked like cells in a prison camp, and very awkward access for the equipment trucks that brought the band's gear up a very narrow alley to the area backstage. The room itself was wide and shallow, with standing room in front of the stage where it sat against the alley wall, a bank of risers opposite on the Clarkson Street wall, a sound booth at the top of the risers and a catwalk to the light booth that was suspended from the ceiling out over the audience.

There was a concession stand under an archway at the north end of the room near the entrance on Clarkson, where, on opening night when Jethro Tull was playing, a cook on some sort of bad trip began stabbing himself in the chest with a butcher knife, which suggested to many of us that the mojo in the place was maybe not what one would hope it to be. Other than that sordid kitchen and some very overtaxed restrooms, there was not much in the way of amenities of any sort. The difficulties there were compounded by the fact there was no parking whatsoever, so if you lived too far away to walk to the show, you parked on the streets wherever you could find a spot and hoped your vehicle was still there when you returned.

It is a measure of how badly the people of Denver wanted to hear the music that Green had no trouble selling out the shows. After all, Denver's big time venue in those days was the Denver Coliseum, which was the perfect place to have animals hogtied by cowboys and broncos busted, but was much less conducive to concerts, where the sound bounced around that concrete palace relentlessly and emerged as something only vaguely related to what the band was playing. Despite its demeanor, Mammoth Gardens was no worse than the other venues in town you were accustomed to, none of which to date gave patrons much of anything of quality except the music and the light shows. Here at least the sound was good.

So, in the very brief eight months of its existence, Mammoth Gardens packed 'em in, show after show, for acts like Jimi Hendrix, the Grateful Dead, the Doors, Joe Cocker, Johnny Winter, Procol Harum, Santana, Eric Burdon and War, Spirit, John Hammond, Poco, Van Morrison, the Nitty Gritty Dirt Band, Flash Cadillac, Zephyr, 60,000,000 Buffalo, and the very best concert you ever saw in all those years, not once but two nights in a row, that was forever after known simply as The Who at Mammoth Gardens.

On June 9 and 10, 1970, you sat in the back of the club on the risers for a while and then made your way past the sound booth and up the catwalk to the light booth. Charlie Morrell was there, Dan Fong was there, the light guys were there, and you were joined at one time or another those two nights by every spirit from every corner of the unseen realms, all in full regalia. The Who came out blazing through their hits, one after another, no pause, no hesitation. The sound was thundering. The memory of Dali's Crucifixion came to you from out of the blue. You felt like you were pinned to the wall. Halfway through the show, Roger Daltrey announced they were going to debut their latest work, and they launched into a full blown performance of Tommy (can you hear me?) It was purely and simply an incredible show. Twice.

There was precious little that you and Barry Fey ever agreed on, but if you asked him, as many did, what was the finest show of the hundreds of concerts he produced, his answer was immediate and never varied in all those years. "The Who at Mammoth Gardens," he would say. "No question."

Stuart Green and his concert hall lasted not very long at all. In one of Denver's worst neighborhoods, on Colfax Avenue, it's most fabled, crime-ridden street, Mammoth Gardens was deemed a detriment to Capitol Hill. In just eight months, some pretty good concerts were presented and among them the single best show ever. Then it was gone. Don't fight the law, Stu. Barry coulda told ya.

There were people promoting concerts at CU, like Kent Lewis, Phil Lobel and Doug Brunkow of the Program Council, who put on some great shows, and later on, Kenny Weissberg, who left second wave KRNW-FM for San Diego, where he carved out a successful career for himself with the next wave of rockers, but first there were guys like Marty Wolff and Kit Thomas, who were dreaming of the big time.

A red-haired, super bright, and very competent young guy named Dick Kreck, who was an editor at The Denver Post and later would become a very successful columnist wily enough to make a 40 year career from a widely read column he wrote about t-shirts and beer, was a graduate of the same journalism school that produced John Burks, one of the original triumvirate with the great Ralph Gleason and Jann Wenner who ran Rolling Stone magazine, which was a black and white rag in those days.

Burks asked Kreck who asked you to look into the Rocky Mountain Pop Festival (or whatever it was called that particular day), which supposedly was happening that coming summer somewhere high in the Rockies under the auspices of promoters nobody ever had heard of. So you wended your way to a fine old home on 14th and Pine or thereabouts in Boulder, where you met with Marty Wolff and Kit Thomas and a half-dozen other very hip and very long-haired guys, who were talking up a music festival everybody was gonna play.

Who? You name it. Beatles, Stones, Jimi, Janis, The Who, the Doors, just to name a few. Did they have contracts? Well, no, but it was going to be so big, so many people were coming, those bands would have to play. The people would *demand* it.

Well, maybe not, and that one flamed out fast, but they were just some of the local guys reaching for that stage, the big stage, where fame and a few bucks could be had.

Phil Lobel was for years part of the Feyline/Chuck Morris team. Wolff got pretty far down that road, too. He and Thomas put on some good shows in Boulder in the early days, especially the Balls For Peace series of concerts at CU, and a number of other concerts that may have been with or without Thomas as co-producer. Not sure. Either way, Marty was a force in bringing live music to the Boulder scene, and later on he had the good sense to get close to Fey early on and pick off some of the smaller gigs in learning the nuances of the trade.

There was a time when he modeled himself on Chip Monck, and much later on with All Star Lighting, he lit up the Doobie Brothers tours. He ended up in L.A. where he nearly made it big many times, but not quite. Finally, though, he made enough money in other ventures to move to Maui, become a wildlife photographer working underwater and commenced to dealing with an altogether different kettle of fish.

Mountain w/Leslie West and Felix Pappalardi at Norlin LIbrary — Marty Wolff standing far left

16

GASSED

BARRY FEY WAS GETTING BIGGER. The business was beginning to boom. Before there was Woodstock, there was the Denver Pop Festival in June of 1969. This one was for real. It was possibly the first time a single promoter tackled an event of that scale. All the highs and lows of rock & roll enterprise were manifest at Mile High Stadium that weekend. The bands were a mixed bag, the music ranged in quality from the extraordinary to Iron Butterfly, and the crowds were pretty big. But the real story was the battle at the gates.

You had interviews lined up with Frank Zappa, Big Mama Thornton, and Jimi Hendrix, so it was looking like an interesting weekend. After weeks of rain, the weather was beautiful, the field was bright green and glistening, the stage was set up facing the west stands with maybe 40 yards of grass between the band and the fans, and the stars looked to be aligned.

But the gate crashers were aligned, too. By now, the "music should be free" crowd had hardened into a free-floating band of anarchists who made the scene at every concert of any consequence and baited the police. The cops were more than happy to respond and battle after battle ensued. The gate crashers had a knee-jerk sort of sympathy working for them from many in the crowds who instinctively distrusted the "pigs." It wasn't like Jimi was playing for nothing, more like $50,000, in fact, guaranteed up front, but the musicians had a pass. It was the promoters who took the heat. It was their gates that were crashed.

You had that backstage pass that came with the newspaper gig and you moved from where the bands gathered to the stage sometimes and the stands at others. Friday night you had the pleasure of meeting with Big Mama Thornton after her set and were suitably wowed by this charming woman who'd been gigging for longer than you'd been alive. "Can I ask you something personal," you said, and

Big Mama Thornton

she replied, "What's that?" with just a little skepticism. "You ever get tired of all this attention," you said, waving your hand toward the stands off in the distance. She looked at you with eyes wide, shook her head just once, and said, "Nope. Like the money, too."

There was noise enough between sets to make it obvious the gate crashers and the cops were at it outside, but inside the Festival, everything was pretty cool. Frank Zappa played the crowd like a bandleader, at one point having everybody stand up, sit down, lean one way, wave your arms another way, the band behind him vamping the whole time, until he finally silenced them, shook his head, and asked the crowd, "Do you do everything you're told?"

For a crowd that was inclined to applaud "In-a-gadda-da-vida" during the following set, it was a question worth asking. Even with the riots to come, when you think back on the Festival, Iron Butterfly was the low point, a downer of a way to close opening night.

Hope springs eternal, and there was a lot to look forward to on Saturday. The lineup included Zephyr, Poco, Johnny Winter, and Creedence Clearwater Revival, which was a big step up from last night's close. Plus, you got to talk to Frank Zappa, who turned out to be an extraordinarily bright and very funny guy.

You met him for a late breakfast at his hotel downtown before his flight back to L.A. When you met and shook hands, he looked at your feet and said, "Brown shoes?" "Don't make it," you replied. He gave you some insight into dealing with a pro. Unlike so many musicians you met with, most of whom were suffering the very first pangs of stardom and a little financial success, Zappa was gracious and charming without the least bit of obsequiousness or arrogance, the conjoined twins of rock & roll stardom. He treated you with respect. You were doing your job, your job had value, and he expected the same respect from you, for the same reason.

By the time you got to Mile High, the storm clouds were gathering. Not the weather, which was excellent, but large crowds of very rowdy long-haired folks and cops in riot gear. There was the smell of trepidation in the air.

You have to remember that all this was something new. Crowds of this size at concerts had happened at Newport, where everyone was cool and extremely well behaved, and at Monterey, which was at the absolute apex of love and peace as an orienting ethic. Nobody at the time had heard of stadium shows and nobody, including Fey, his staff, the police, and the crowds, none of them had a frame of reference in deciding what it all meant and how to deal with it.

But the show went on. A band called Aeorta opened the show and on your best day with your life on the line, you couldn't summon a recollection of who they were. But Zephyr came next and that's when everything imploded. Outside, in the trenches, DPD decided that tear gas was in order, a not uncommon choice of weapons in these pitched battles they fought with unruly crowds. They shot a few canisters of it at the people who were crashing the gates.

If you are a native Coloradan, or even someone who's lived here for a while, you know at any given moment on any particular day, the wind blows west to east, traveling down the face of the mountain front and out on to the plains. So it was this Saturday as Colorado's favorite local band began to play.

The cops and the gates and the people who crashed them were on the Federal Boulevard side of Mile High Stadium. The audience, many thousands of fans, were to the east of them. And the wind, however gently, blew.

"Cross the River," Candy Givens was singing, when a thick cloud of pepper gas wafted through the crowd and onto the field where the stage was set. One moment the audience was bopping up and down in rhythm; the next, they were convulsing, gasping, crying, stumbling over the seats, over each other, rubbing their eyes with their fists, trying to escape.

They poured over the low wall that separated the stands from the field. By the hundreds, then the thousands, they blundered their way toward the stage. Blinded, crying, some of them vomiting. It was a terrible moment of confusion and panic.

Zephyr, Denver, CO 1969 / courtesy: David Givens

"Lie down," Candy yelled at them through the mic. "Cover your face with your shirt, don't rub your eyes." David Givens recalls that she invited the crowd to the front of the stage, and "...swept her outstretched arm left to right towards the hundreds of people crowding onto the turf down in front of us and they all dropped as if she had shot them. Then she said to them, 'Well, since we're already crying, let's do some blues.' She called for 'St. James Infirmary,' ...the crowd relaxed and all was well."

Much as you always admired her, you never were more proud of Candy than how she handled herself and the stage that day. What happened was bad, very dangerous, and it was miraculous that no one was seriously hurt. Her composure, even as she, too, was being blinded and gagged by the gas, made all the difference. She saved Barry's ass that day. Don't know that he ever returned the favor.

The show must go on and so it did. You have but a dim memory of the rest of it. The battle outside was raging. It just went on and on. The music became an afterthought, which when you think about it as you often have is a terrible way to summarize a music festival.

Fey told you later that his plan was to open the gates on Sunday when the show began and let everybody in for free. Seemed like a good idea at the time but the cops said, "No!" They saw it as a concession they weren't willing to make. So the battle began again on Sunday. Fey and his staff tried to circumvent the cops by passing out tickets to the crowd. They quickly learned the gate crashers didn't want to get in, free or not. They just wanted to fight.

It's hard to remember the music. Some of it must have been good. But it became a subset to the larger, bolder, badder concert playing out in the streets.

There are two memories that do persist. One is Joe Cocker, who played what was for him a relatively tepid set on Sunday after hiding in the locker rooms under the stands for most of the afternoon before he went on. He told you years later when you talked about it that he was scared to death and couldn't stop thinking, "these fockin' Americans are insane."

The other is your interview with Jimi Hendrix, sitting in a van behind the stage after he and the Experience closed the festival Sunday night. By then, the worst of the violence was spent, the gate crashers who hadn't been arrested had gone home, the cops were worn out, their taste for battle sated.

Jimi didn't do bad shows. He'd been on the circuit for years as a sideman in various R&B bands, so he knew enough to appreciate the opportunity and he made it count. You knew him vaguely from a conversation or two the night he played Regis College and then showed up to jam with Tommy Bolin at the Dog. You assume that his show was superior, though in truth, you don't remember it.

What you do remember is the vibe in the van that night, when Jimi and Noel Redding and Mitch Mitchell each had so little to say and the tension was thick; and, first Redding and then Mitchell excused himself and disappeared into the night. And, Jimi Hendrix, the one and only, smoked the rest of a joint with you and shrugged and seemed to be saying: hey, man, figure it out for yourself. It was the last time the Jimi Hendrix Experience ever played a gig together.

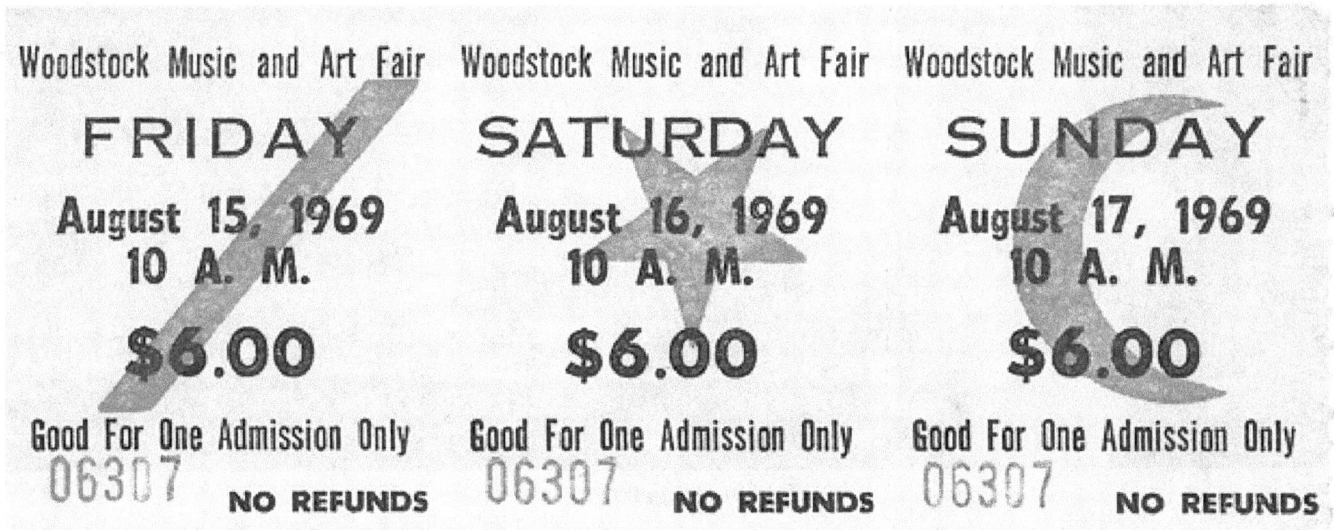

Woodstock Music and Art Fair	Woodstock Music and Art Fair	Woodstock Music and Art Fair
FRIDAY	SATURDAY	SUNDAY
August 15, 1969	August 16, 1969	August 17, 1969
10 A. M.	10 A. M.	10 A. M.
$6.00	$6.00	$6.00
Good For One Admission Only	Good For One Admission Only	Good For One Admission Only
06307 NO REFUNDS	06307 NO REFUNDS	06307 NO REFUNDS

Later that summer, a little event called Woodstock happened. The word everywhere was that it was going to be big, a helluva show. You shouldn't miss it. You told your editors at the Post it was gonna be awesome. You should be there. They said they'd think about it. Ran it through channels, came back with an offer: we'll split the cost to send you there. You told them to stuff it. On the 17th of August, every newspaper in the country, if not the world, was covering the story. The important papers had people on site. Not the Post. Not you. But they finally began to get the message. If people hadn't noticed yet that something rather huge and profound was happening, they knew it now.

Keef in Denver 1972

17

BIG STONES

THE BIGGEST ACT OF THEM ALL IN 1969, the Rolling Stones, was heading out on the road in North America for a month long series of arena and stadium shows, two per day in many of the cities along the way. Nobody ever had done that before. Festivals with a fistful of bands over several days could fill a stadium, but one band with an opening act?

The Stones were about to prove it could be done. They were going to put a stake in the ground in America that like a totem forever after would define the image of rock & roll stardom and the visage of the rock star. This tour would shape the mythos of sex, drugs, and rock & roll as the calling card of the culture.

In 1969, there was nothing to refer to in planning an event like this. No precedent. Nothing of this scale had been done. Nobody knew for certain how to do it or whether it would work.

The Beatles in 1965 had done 15 shows in 10 cities, with abominable sound, a catch as catch can approach to the planning and execution, and one stop along the way, The Beatles at Shea Stadium, that played to 55,000 fans, none of whom heard anything but each other screaming, and grossed more than $300,000, which suggested there was serious potential to be realized.

The Stones made it happen. By the time it was completed, the ground rules would be written, what was needed would be known, the way to do it proven out, the dos and don'ts would have been established through trial and error. But this tour would be created from whole cloth. A lot of mistakes were made. The promotion was full of screw-ups. The accommodations were erratic. These were the days when backstage was locker rooms with cement floors and wooden benches. Food? Maybe a bag of chips and a case of cheap beer. There was nothing 'luxe about it, but it was a lesson learned. Somehow, the shows were very good in spite of it all, except the last one. The music got done.

Maybe Barnum & Bailey had a sense of how to put on a circus like this, but it existed nowhere in the annals of rock & roll to date, not even in our wildest imagination. It was THE tour that showed the way for all the subsequent ventures on the road in the rock & roll arcade. It was big news, a very big deal. The future was being rolled out. Trouble was, sorry Barry, Denver was not on the itinerary.

But Barry Fey was not about to let that snub go down. He got on the phone with the Stones' people and finally, after much wrangling and swearing and pleading and the persuasiveness for which he became so well known, the world's greatest rock band added a "warm-up" show to their North American tour in Moby Gym at CSU in Fort Collins, the best venue he could get on short notice.

Fort Collins in those days was still pretty rural, CSU not all that long removed from its day as Colorado A&M, as in agriculture and mining. The local yokels in their shit-kickers and cowboy hats lined the courtyard outside the arena that evening, commenting loud and long through fat cheeks full of chew about "them hippies" and all the perfunctory questions: whether "that's a boy or a girl?" and the inevitable judgment that the long-haired guy is "the ugliest chick I've ever seen."

With that as the setting for opening the tour, and considering how it ended a month later, it was perhaps auspicious that the show went off so well. This tour initiated the era of big-time rock & roll. The venues were larger, the audiences bigger, the sound system and lighting markedly better than any that had gone before. The tour was produced from start to finish by one guy, Ronnie Schneider, who created the model for financing the tours by capturing every aspect of the cash flow: up-front deposits from the local promoters, ticket sales, and all the ancillary rights to revenue from t-shirts, posters and the like.

It used to be that bands toured to promote their record sales. That's where the money was. On the road, they were lucky to break even and mostly tried to not lose their ass. This tour began to change all that. There would come a time, maybe it was the Steel Wheels tour in 1989 or perhaps Voodoo Lounge in 1994, when Mick would tell you the band was grossing $95 million on concessions alone. That was 20 or 25 years later, but this road show began the long, true arc toward that time.

The tour thereafter went west to east. Maybe you flew to L.A. for the next two shows, and to Oakland for the two after that. It was a 24/7 party, non-stop for 5 days, and after the fifth show you were exhausted. Screwed, blued and tattooed is probably the way to put it. An absolutely phenomenal time that wrung you out and put you up still pretty wet. You were 24, strong as an ox, and nearly unable to find your way home, you were so tired. The Stones had a month to go.

Show after show, day after day, they did it. One great performance after another. These guys weighed about 50 pounds each on a good day and yet you came to think of them as perhaps the toughest guys in the world.

Many people in the business came and went, some of them way too soon, and when they died, Brian, Jimi, Janis, Jim Morrison, and so many others, the founders of the 27 Club, it was sad but not surprising. They lived at a pace that simply wasn't sustainable.

If you had to guess one person who definitely would not make it, Keith Richards would have been an excellent candidate. There was a time in the early '70s that he was virtually translucent. But survive he did and prosper. Keef is unanimously regarded by those in the know as the single coolest dude ever. Through all the ups and downs, he has made great music and run a great band for more than 50 years. And just for laughs, he also wrote the best autobiography by a rock musician that has ever been penned. As recently as last week, he was quoted in the Wall Street Journal as saying, "I'm not gonna live forever. Not even me." But, if he did, you would not be especially surprised.

So, when you saw him in '72 on tour, before the verdict was in, and Keith was deep in the stuff, you wondered if he would make it. The shows night after night were awesome, and like the time three years before, you did a small part of the circuit with them and nearly died of exhaustion. This time around, the Stones knew what to do, how to handle it. Last time out, they were trying to prove themselves and the concept. This time, they were rock & roll royalty. Everybody bowed down. This was by proclamation The World's Greatest Rock & Roll Band.

They did 52 shows in 31 cities in less than two months, including both an afternoon and an evening show in Denver, both of which sold out. It was a feat of unprecedented showmanship, sheer endurance, and phenomenal success. The tour grossed around $4 million, nearly $25 million in today's dollars. It attracted the first wave of celebrity hangers on, people like

Truman Capote, Lee Radziwill, Dick Cavett, Andy Warhol, Terry Southern, and god knows who all, the flock of pigeons thinking themselves swans who smell the first vestiges of big fame, big money, big ITness, and flock to it like a church steeple they soon enough will cover with their droppings. It was wet with possibilities.

But, too, in nearly every city, at nearly every show, the battle outside is raging. Gate crashers and riot police battled, ticket forgers caused big problems, drug busts were rampant in the audiences as well as at the scene outside the gates. Many dozens of people were arrested in the course of that tour as similar scenes played out in city after city.

Peace and love had always been a tenuous proposition. Some thought it already had been sacrificed on the altar at Altamont, where it suffered death by Angels. You thought about it a lot, how viable it really was in a world so complex, so deeply seated in competition, control, comeuppance. It was an appeal to our better selves, which weren't always or even often in evidence. To some, in fact, aspiring to those selves was thought to be only a posture.

The Rolling Stones version 3, 1975

It was easier to write about the Fifties and Sixties, because you were young then and everything was a source of wonder. By the Seventies, you were an adult, but you weren't really ready to put away childish things. You weren't at all certain what was proposed as "getting real" was something you were willing to accept. Dreams die hard when they finally fail you, but so far you were still dreaming.

The Ride

18

IN THE DAY

S O, YOU TURNED ON THE RADIO first thing in the morning in maybe 1970 or '71, right at
11:00 o'clock or so, the glorious Sandy Phelps was playing some tunes, you took a shower,
brushed your teeth, tied your freak flag into a pony tail, pulled on some clothes, and go. Maybe
you dropped by Mother's Café on the Hill for a stack of great pancakes, some eggs and hash
browns, as only Roscoe can make 'em; or on alternate days, you took in some serious breakfast
at the Bakery on 14th, where the cinnamon rolls with raisins, currants and nuts were scary
good and the omelets soft and fluffy.

Full with all that good food, you stop by Martin's Western Wear to pick up your new pair of Stuart boots, custom made for you in Tucson, Arizona, gas up the car at Walter Finger's Fina out on North Broadway just past the school, and slowly wend your way up beautiful Sunshine Canyon to the Gold Hill Inn for a delicious late lunch prepared by Barbara and Frank Finn.

You follow lunch and a smoke with a long, leisurely drive up Left Hand Canyon and blast around the curves in the '63 Porche 356 S90 roadster across the Peak to Peak Highway, up the St. Vrain past Allen's Park for an afternoon fishing at Sheeps Lake on Fall River Road in Rocky Mountain National Park.

And later, when you finally had worked up a bit of an appetite again, you would roll through Estes Park and head back down the canyon to La Chaumière for another of the many fabulous dinners you enjoyed there over the years. Then the drive down to Lyons, and across the narrow two lane blacktop of Highway 36 all the way south to where the sign on the north end of town welcomed you back to Boulder. Stay and Play, it said. That was a day in the life in the day.

When Pearl was a street; mid-Sixties Boulder / credit: Carnegie Library for Local History

More days than not, though, you worked and played in town. Dot's Diner for breakfast, Tom's Tavern or the Broken Drum for lunch and a beer, or maybe Don's Cheese and Sausage Mart for a sandwich. Dinner at the Catacombs or the IndoCeylon Restaurant in the Boulderado Hotel, where at Fleur d' Lis, Tim Combs, the future mayor of Lyons, also served a very fine brunch.

Me and Henry / credit: Carnegie Library for Local History

Maybe you'd pick up a loaf of bread from the Sanitary Bakery for breakfast toast tomorrow. Or drop into Fred's for simple fare at lunch. For drinks maybe J.J. McCabe's, right around the corner from Oraivi, past the Firestone Tire store and Phantasmagoria, where Lawry and Cathy Covell sold their leather goods, years before they moved on to Denver and very high fashion; and, where in that two story room at the bar the Naropa guru Trumpa Rimpoche held court, having a great time pouring beer from his booth upstairs on people at the tables below, as you supposed the holy men are prone to do; or, often it was the Walrus, Potters, or any of the other places that began to spring up all over town.

Everywhere you were, in Boulder, in Denver, there was always the music. It was the soundtrack of your life, on the radio, on your turntable, and in every juke joint in town. It was so good for so long that maybe it crossed your mind a time or two it was too good to last.

...goo goo g'joob credit: Carnegie Library for Local History

Led Zeppelin U.S. debut, Denver, CO 1968

19

ROCKS ROLLED

ONE RESULT OF ALL THOSE FESTIVALS in the late '60s is that tours were about to get very big. The Stones got it started in '69, but there already were signs of what was to come. Fey was putting on shows at the Auditorium Arena, which was small but nice, and the Denver Coliseum, a rodeo arena made of a cement oval with a dirt floor over which temporary flooring was laid. It was a dump that did no favors to the bands or the audience, and it presented huge challenges to Magnum Opus Sound, John Brosnahan's company, which made the best of it and produced pretty good sound in absolutely dreadful conditions. Like throwing a steel barrel of crystal goblets down a stairwell. And broadcasting it.

The shows were cobbled together from name acts that Fey pretty skillfully chose, a little of this and a little of that, who gets top billing, who plays second, and some unknown band to open the show. He sold out every one of them. People wanted to hear the music. If the Coliseum is where it was playing, that's where they're going.

You saw them all and they were a mixed bag. A glaring example was one of the first in 1968, when Vanilla Fudge was headlining and Spirit was second billed. Some no name band from England opened the show.

When they came on stage, you looked them over and, hey, wait a minute, that's Jimmy Page! The Yardbirds had always been one of your favorite bands, and Page was the third of that many great guitarists who played lead for them at one time or another, the others being Eric Clapton and Jeff Beck.

That night, Led Zeppelin made its debut in the United States, playing for $750, and they absolutely destroyed the place. It was an incandescent moment in time, the arrival of a monster act, and nobody who saw and heard their set will ever forget it. Not one of them ever doubted for a minute that this was a band to be reckoned with, one that would define the next wave of rock & roll.

How Spirit or Vanilla Fudge managed to play after what Zep laid on the audience is hard to imagine, let alone remember. What you do remember is a year later, they were back in Denver playing for Fey at the Coliseum and he told you, "They held me up for $25 grand! I can't keep paying these prices. They're gonna break me."

What you both could foresee in the not to distant future, if you dared take a look, is the day when Led Zeppelin wouldn't walk across the hall for $25 grand, let alone blow the room away. Because the music was about to become a very big business. But that was later, too, and there was still a lot of music to be made, just for the sheer pleasure of playing, to make a few bucks, and to satisfy that craving we all had to hear and be heard.

Many another great band played concerts in that concrete tomb, including The Who, Crosby, Stills and Nash, and the Rolling Stones, among others. It was an embarrassment of riches in an embarrassment of a hall. Denver was known far and wide for the enthusiasm of its fans; probably, too, for providing one of the worst venues in America to play.

The tragedy was that one of the finest facilities in the world, Red Rocks Amphitheater, was just a short distance away. But the city fathers in their wisdom had ruled it off limits for anything as tawdry as rock & roll. Riots, you know.

You had been present at all three of them. None had been much fun. When Ray Charles finally came on stage in 1962, after keeping a moody crowd of maybe 7,000 sunbleached and alcohol-fueled people waiting for hours, he claimed to have been stuck in traffic but likely was stuck with a needle, and used the surliness of the crowd as an excuse to play a very brief set. News reports to the contrary, your memory is maybe three or four songs - a half dozen tops and he said, "That's it." Torrents of beer bottles flew stageward, Pogo Poge ran for shelter, and broken glass rose in tiers before your weary eyes.

Aretha Franklin was a great talent but like many performers of her era was deeply suspicious about getting screwed by promoters. Experience don't forget. Most acts demanded cash up front before they went on stage. When she arrived at Red Rocks in 1968 and a nearly full house awaited her show, something wasn't right. The cash wasn't there. She yelled and screamed. Then she walked on stage and announced to the crowd, she wasn't gonna play. No show tonight. Ain't gonna happen. Another night, another riot.

Burly Bill McNichols, who became mayor of Denver that same year after his predecessor quit to run Continental Airlines and who held office with a vice-like grip until failure to clean up a snowstorm that left the city paralyzed for nearly a week in the early Eighties cost him his job, had a simple if ultimately untenable and thoroughly ignorant solution: ban rock & roll from Red Rocks. A lot of people, Barry Fey foremost among them, take credit for ultimately undoing his ban. Maybe you should take a small bow, as well.

Having learned a little bit about the way power was wielded by the Fourth Estate, you took the initiative to write a couple of articles that compared the use of city facilities in Denver, such as the Coliseum and convention center, with those of other cities in the West. Denver didn't fare well. Very poorly, actually.

As the first rock & roll writer in the long history of The Denver Post, your work was very heavily redlined by editors, who allowed you virtually no quarter to discuss the subject at hand. Murder, rape, mayhem were perfectly suitable fare, but sex, drugs, and rock & roll were not fit for a family newspaper.

This series about Denver's use of its venues, though, was right up the snout of this rooting porcine creature. Like foraging for truffles in the woods. This was muckraking, a time honored tradition. It ran almost untouched by the news desk and it definitely got some attention.

Soon enough, you were summoned to Miss Bonfils' office. The Bonfils family ran the Post throughout its somewhat storied history and Helen Bonfils was currently in charge. Seated around the large oval table in her conference room were the paper's bigwigs, Charles Buxton and Bill Hornby, Miss Helen herself, and the Mayor, along with Sam Feiner, Director of Theaters and Arenas. Miss Helen and you were the only two whose hair reached your shoulders. Yours was a little longer.

After thoroughly berating you for the damage your articles were causing the city's reputation in the convention trade, a nearly apoplectic Feiner finally shut up when Hornby unexpectedly noted that the articles were thoroughly researched and the information appeared to be accurate. The Mayor cleared his throat, Feiner glared, and Hizzoner, after looking around the table, as though sizing up what there was to be gained and lost in this miasmic bout with some hippie writer, finally looked at you and said, "What exactly do you want?"

"Open up Red Rocks to rock & roll," you said. And they did. Fey had a suit against them for restraint of trade, which was certainly a factor. Even the straight businessmen in town, if asked, probably were questioning why this rich new revenue stream called rock & roll was being suppressed. Doubtless there were many reasons for the decision. Success has many parents while failure is an orphan. But politicians get very nervous when the press turns against them. Cherished beliefs and staunch positions vanish in the wind.

You took a certain satisfaction from the wrap up to the meeting, as all the suits were kissing and making up, genuflecting to each other, so glad to have found a reasonable solution and pretty much ignoring you, who after all wasn't really worth their time beyond whatever nuisance you proved to be, when the regal Miss Bonfils herself, a denizen and angel for many years of Broadway theater and perhaps therefore less disturbed by your appearance than the rest, looked at you briefly with a twinkle in her eye and the slightest smile on her face, nodded once and left the room.

Very soon thereafter, in June of 1971, Jethro Tull played Red Rocks, the first rock concert there in three years, and very quickly, too, another riot ensued. A sold out crowd was in attendance. Another thousand or more gathered in the area outside the gates. Gatecrashing

by now was a well-honed sport for a certain breed of characters who set out to create mayhem at concerts wherever they were held. They attacked the gates, the police reacted, the battle ensued.

You had no expertise in crowd control, but having been tear-gassed now on numerous occasions, mostly for trying to have a night on the town and hear some tunes, you came to question the wisdom of firing teargas in the vicinity of very large crowds of mostly peaceful people at outdoor venues who had paid for their tickets and were there to enjoy the show. Teargas drifts. It is powerful. Disorienting. Nauseating. And when, as it did that night and as it had almost exactly two years before at the Denver Pop Festival, it drifted into the crowd, a very dangerous situation unfolded.

Some people claimed the police had purposely shot teargas canisters into the theater. It would fit neatly as a conspiracy by the City to show once again that these hooligans aren't fit to use a beautiful public facility. But Leslie Haseman, who is reliable beyond any question, told you she was there outside the gates and that the gate crashers were the ones who lobbed the canisters over the wall and into the crowd.

The stands and the stage were saturated with teargas, which took some time to disperse. The band very reasonably could have refused to play, which would have incited a riot inside the arena as well as outside. But, Ian Anderson saved the day. He was calm, collected, soothing. He talked, he sang, he played, he brought everything under control in a way that earned the praise of even the police, who knew he had redirected what was shaping up as a disaster.

It was another concert where you remember more about the mayhem than you do about the music. And, when it was over, everyone went home, battered but not too terribly the worse for wear, you went to bed after writing about it and awoke to learn the City once again was banning rock & roll at Red Rocks.

So, the Rolling Stones, The Who, Led Zeppelin never played what is one of the finest concert venues in the world. Instead, they played a concert each in succeeding years at the Denver Coliseum, a truly embarrassing option for which the fans of Denver can thank the obdurate Mayor McNichols and his political machine.

By the time Fey had created the Summer of Stars and the city finally had seen the light, those acts were too big to play there. Red Rocks seats 10,000 or so; by then, those two bands were playing stadiums of 50,000 to 100,000 fans. The economics of Red Rocks simply didn't work for them anymore.

There is a story that many years later, not too long in fact before he died, Fey was trying to book The Who at Red Rocks, with tickets contemplated to cost in four figures each and the likelihood that even at those prices it would sell out. The prospect is intriguing to think about, embodying as it does both the deep allure of the music they make and the sky high cost of presenting it in this day and age.

It also embodies a sad truth: towering as his reputation, sterling as his track record, solid as his relationships with the bands and their managers, there was simply no way Barry Fey was going to get it done. The business had long since moved on. The shows these days were put on by Live Nation or by AEG. They didn't have room for independents anymore, whatever your former status. The bands played where they booked them, or they didn't play at all.

You can't help but imagine how fine a night under the stars might have been, amidst those mighty sandstone slabs in the thrall of its perfect acoustics, hearing and seeing any of the three mightiest rock bands of their time, or of any time for that matter. It was not to be. You saw a lot of great shows there before the Seventies came to a close, but the ones that got away too often are the ones that linger in the mind.

Marcello Cabus, Jr., the author, Tony Funches, Denver early '70s

---

20

PEEPS

L ESLIE HASEMAN WAS A BRIGHT, beautiful, engaging woman who was Barry Fey's personal assistant from the earliest days of Feyline, Inc., when she, Cindy Fey, and Cathy Millward were the only women in the office. In the rock & roll maelstrom fast filling up with cute young boys in high heeled boots and way too much testosterone for their own good, there was one thing everyone of them learned sooner or later. Don't. Mess. With. Leslie! Those who did came to regret it very quickly, later to remark on the sense of their entire life passing before their eyes in the time it took her to read them the riot act and put them firmly in their place. Leslie took no shit from you or anybody else, no matter how lofty your place in the pantheon of rock stars or the fists full of dollars you might represent.

She was nobody's fool. Ornery as Barry Fey could be, most people went to him with their problems because it was easier than getting crossways with her. Leslie was a person who was exceedingly gracious and kind to the low-key types they dealt with, and very sharp-tongued and profane with those who were too full of themselves. She also was the only one who kept Barry at bay.

Like every other guy in town, you were totally taken with her. Like every other guy, you hit on her more than once. Like all the rest of them, she turned you down. Many years later, in talking about those days, she explained that she knew if she gave in to even one of you, there'd be no end of it in fending off the rest. If she slept with you, how in the hell could she handle Jagger or Daltry?

She could tell you story after story about one tour and another, the legions of whacked out musicians and roadies and groupies that peopled her life in those days, and many of them were hysterically funny and some just plain sad. But one of them involved Keith Moon and his "needs" that he asked her to attend, and it was the only time you ever saw her beautiful brown face turn nearly scarlet red.

She handled it, of course, as she always did, calling in one of the many groupies who were always about and providing her with the key to yet another encounter with a legend, one with unsurpassed rhythm, no less, but the mere memory of it was enough to remind Leslie very vividly of all the minefields she negotiated with such skill, grace, and ferocious determination.

Many, many years later, at the memorial service for a beautiful woman who died way too young, you gave the eulogy and afterwards, while the emotions were still churning, Leslie put her arms around you, kissed you lightly on the lips, and said, "That was beautiful. I have to go, but I'll see you very soon." Less than a month later, she was dead of a massive stroke. You never saw her again. May she rest in peace.

One fine day late in 1969, right around Christmas, while you and every other long-hair were trying to absorb the meaning of Altamont, that final, fatal stop on the Stones' tour last fall that began rather gloriously in Fort Collins and ended tragically at a race track in California, and that ever thereafter was thought of as the far side of the Summer of Love, the day that love and peace suffered death by Angels, the doorbell at your place in Denver rang and when you answered it, this rather amazing character was there.

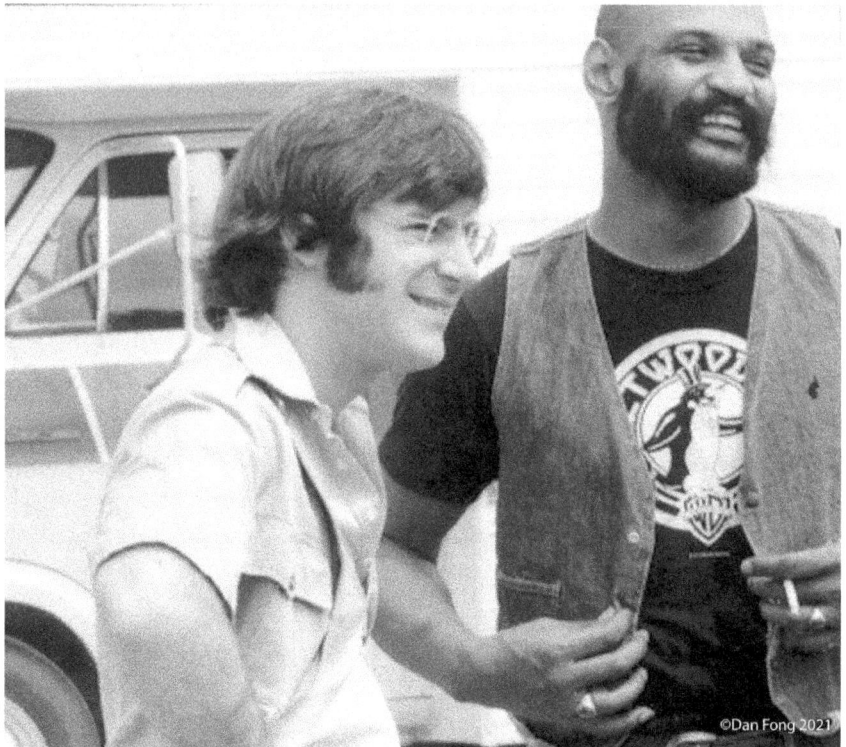

John Sebastian and Tony Funches

He looked like a cross between an Ethiopian prince and a panther, about six and a quarter feet tall, maybe 250 pounds of very lean muscle, a short Afro and sparkling eyes. His name was Tony Funches, he said, "and Barry said maybe I could stay here for a while."

"Let me ask you something," you said through the screen door, "aren't you the guy that was punching out the Angels at Altamont?" He said that he was. "Aren't you afraid they're coming after you?" He said he wasn't afraid of them. You allowed as how maybe you were.

That's how you and Tony became roommates. "Let me get my stuff," he said, went out to his car, returned with a duffle bag and three Dobermanns. It would be nearly a year before you ever went out in your own back yard again.

You stayed in a big old place on 19th and Albion, just a block from City Park, which was a great place for walking off the hangover from the night before. There were quite a few to walk off.

Lots of people came by to visit. Baby Huey, a 350 pounder from Chicago, was a regular. He performed stark naked except for a diaper and had on each finger of his hands a ring that held a generous reservoir of cocaine under a pop-up stone. He played a lot of shows in Denver in those years and was, fortunately, a very good natured guy to have around. Wore clothes when he visited, too. He was another singer who barely missed the 27 club, dying the next year at age 26.

Mick Taylor dropped by one day. He showed you one lick after another on guitar, which you played exactly as he had but the sound was nowhere near the same. After several hours, many beers and more than a few joints, he finally leaned over next to you and in his British accent said as graciously as he could, "Perhaps your talents lie in other areas." Tony thought it was hysterical and never missed a chance to remind you of it.

Jim Morrison was a house guest more than once. Tony was his bodyguard at one time and another, so they were pretty tight, and he was seeing a woman who lived on 17th and Oneida, near Colorado Woman's College, which gave him reason to come to town. By then he already was a very big star, maybe the first pre-packaged symbol of what had been a consciously anti-commer-posture in the music business, but Jim was L.A. show biz would out.

He projected a very moody ambiance, the ways of a poet one supposed, and once you all were sitting around, drinking beer, smoking pot, and shooting breeze, stoners on a lovely afternoon of those wonder-rolled in one after another, when Morrison offhand- edly announced, "I've done acid more than 300 times... and every one's been a bummer."

In the quiet that followed, when the room seemed to expand and contract a few times, as if it too was breathing deeply and ruminating with the rest of you, and the words he spoke faded slowly into the marijuana haze like a wah-wah pedal at the end of a song, and finally you couldn't help asking him, "So, um, why do you keep doing it?" He was dead not more than a year later.

You and Tony were friends for nearly 50 years and when he finally passed away unimaginably far off in the future, it felt as though he had been the hallmark at both ends of a magical piece of time. He is missed and irreplaceable. As are those times.

So many people, famous or not, came and went through that place that you were only slightly surprised when Rebecca Jane tapped you on the shoulder one day and said, "Bob Dylan's at the door." You kind of got your cool on and started to say, "Hello," but it was just a Jehovah's Witness who'd come calling. Really kind of looked like him though.

Joe and Delores Hess at home on the plains east of Boulder c. 1970s / credit: Stephen Collector

21

TOWN AND THE CITY

THERE WAS A LOT HAPPENING IN BOULDER and change inevitably was part of it. For a long stretch of the late Sixties and into the mid-Seventies, things felt like they got better and better. The movement toward the exurban seemed to find a happy medium in that little town and all those surrounding environs; out on the edges of the bowl that surrounded it to the east where it broached the Plains, to Lafayette, Louisville, and even clear out to Longmont, there were large patches of mostly country with a lifestyle in places nearer Appalachia than the trés chic little bubble Boulder eventually would become, and comfortable little towns scattered among them; and, due north toward Lyons and the swath of red rock country that rose up from it to the West; and, up all those little canyon roads, Boulder, Sunshine, Lee Hill and Old Stage to Left Hand, and up both forks of the St. Vrain, where one little community after another had settled; even out south to Eldorado Springs, with its fabled rock walls that climbers scaled and its storied swimming pool where so many of us took the plunge, all of that place unfortunately in close proximity to the highly radioactive Rocky Flats. Other than a little plutonium dust, life up there was pretty cool, too.

Although the music was happening everywhere, the local music scene now was much stronger here than Denver. People wanted out of the cities, and that included a lot of the musicians. The Sixties were exhausting if you lived in America's urban environs. Crime, riots, the battle between the established order and the new disrupters, all of it simply wore people out.

Denver began to suffer a deep vibe of Sopers and 'Ludes, a downer way of coping. Better days were ahead, but even bigger issues to confront would accompany them.

Boulder's club scene thrived. People here were still on the ascendency. Feeling good about where they were and what was happening. There was music everywhere, every night of the week. Daytime, too. In the Band Shell, at the Library, the Student Union, the Fieldhouse, the Stadium on campus, at the ranch out on North Broadway just past the place where it merged with 28th and headed for Lyons, really anywhere you could plug in and crank it up, music was being played.

TULAGI'S

presents
it's Fall Schedule:

FREDDIE KING . . . . TONITE thru Sept. 4

JESSIE COLIN YOUNG . . . . Sept. 6th thru 10th
(of the Youngbloods and Friends)

LEO KOTTKE . . . . Sept. 11th & 12th

NEW YORK ROCK ENSEMBLE . . . . Sept. 13th thru 17th

HERBIE HANCOCK . . . . Sept. 18th thru 23rd

JOHN PRINE and STEVE GOODMAN . . . . Sept. 25th thru 30th

LINDA RHONSTADT . . . . Oct. 2nd thru 7th

STONEGROUND & MANCE LIPSCOMB . . . . Oct. 9th thru 14th

DAN HICKS & HIS HOT LICKS . . . . Oct. 17th thru 22nd

COMING LATER THIS FALL:

Doc Watson, Earl Scruggs, Doug Kershaw, The Johnny Otis Show, and many others.

"on the hill" in Boulder

Oh, that Linda Ronstadt, and a cast of thousands ...

It was a manifestation of what everyone was feeling. A celebration being trumpeted. On guitar, piano, drums. You went out many a night and hopped from one club to another, Art's to the Hi-Lo to Shannon's to the Tule, and out to the Good Earth. Everywhere the bands were cooking and the crowds were urging them on.

Tulagi - the Tule - where more 3.2 beer was consumed than any other place in the U.S.
credit: Carnegie Library for Local History

In Denver, after the Dog and Mammoth Gardens folded, the major shows Barry Fey brought to town were happening in a big way, and some small venue concerts like the great Laura Nyro with LaBelle at the Auditorium Theatre in 1972 were sublime, but the club scene was far less vibrant. There were the usual places where cover bands got the folks dancing and not much else to recommend it. Then Chuck Morris finally left Tulagi's and, with Fey, opened up Ebbets Field. When that and KFML converged, Denver took a significant bump upward.

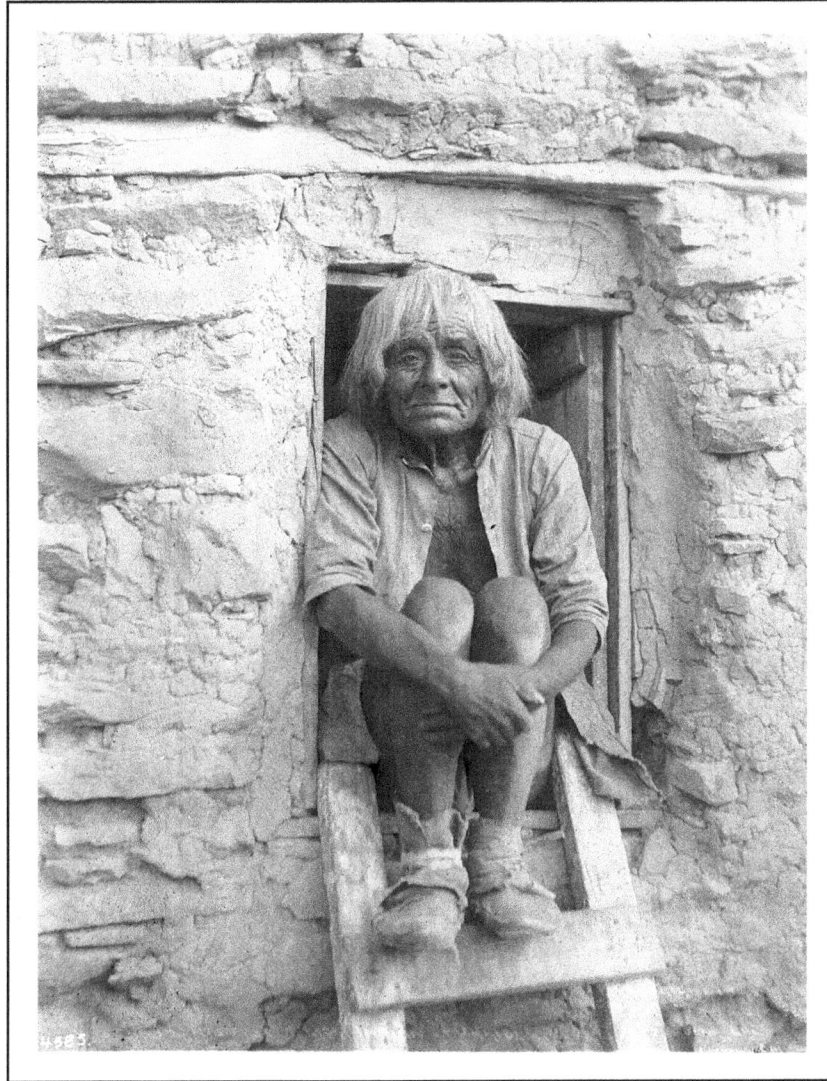

22

MYSTIQUE

DREAMS, DREAMS. From far away, you heard the Pipes of Pan all the way from Morocco, Rock the Casbah; the Baalbek Valley, Indica plants with trunks like trees and music to the rhythm of clomping camel hooves; a night in Tunisia; Arabesque, the call to prayer from the mosques; the caravanserai in the hills of Afghanistan, the tea houses and hookahs and the huts where rugs are woven. Everywhere the sounds of flutes and drums and unnamed stringed instruments, trance music long before you ever heard the term; sadhus with white hashish pollen and songs of reverence; the Taj Mahal by moonlight, sitars and the flutes of snake charmers with the deadly mongoose waiting; the temples and ashrams and Darjeeling; Srinigar, Kashmir and the Gardens of Shalimar; mighty, forbidden Tibet; Kathmandu, Nepal; the lamaseries perched high on the hillsides here in the Himalayas; Jews, Christians, Muslims, Hindis, Sikhs, and Buddhists, all of them strung like beads in a necklace across the cradle of civilization; all of it ancient; all of it a dream and music in it everywhere.

Maybe you needed a break then. Some time away. Like a bad boy in the classroom you sat in a corner with a dunce cap on, eyes closed, thinking about what it all meant, what it was, and what to do about it.

Back in Boulder, after a rest, you worked next door to the Little Kitchen at first and then just up the street in what for years was Snow's Photography Studio, where your gallery on Broad-

way between Walnut and Pearl lit up the street. Bob Musser had a place on 9th and Walnut called Native American Art. Michael and Angela Phillips had a place across the bank parking lot on 13th next to the James Bar that sold all manner of fine Tibetan and other Buddhist art. Between your place and those, there was some truly incredible tribal art to be seen. This wasn't Impressionism, post-Impressionism, Abstract, Minimalist, or Modern art. This was the work those artists learned from.

Many people from all walks of life seemed to be drawn almost instinctively to these unique, highly personal, one-of-a-kind pieces. These were works of a people, many peoples, from a time and place far from the forces that so dominated our days, the relentless commercialism so many were trying to resist, to reform, or merely find a way to live with in order to keep from surrendering. Primitive art, it once was called. Primitive being pre-commercial. It was rare, beautiful, unique, and like so much else, was disappearing. People without knowing why came to experience it, to simply be in its presence.

It was part of that hunger, a persistent craving for new ways of seeing and believing. But, also, it was part of that search for the old ways that were different from what we were raised with, ancient ways that might contain wisdom we were missing and badly needed.

Your gallery began with a family of wooden dolls carved by an Arapahoe or Cheyenne drinking buddy of your long dead Uncle Frank. They'd been in his possession for a long time but he agreed to give them to you as the anchor of your new venture. They were about three feet tall, the baby less than half that, dressed in reservation garb and carved of a hardwood ochered a deep reddish-brown. Inanimate objects sometimes are said to be imbued with spirit. These were fully that. You sat them, father and mother upright and baby lying in her lap, in the back seat of your '61 Cadillac Sedan de Ville and drove back to Boulder from Denver, catching a glimpse more than once of the family in the rearview mirror and noting how very present they were, hearing on the radio "Geronimo's Cadillac" and laughing at how appropriate it seemed.

Not long thereafter, Michael Murphey became a customer (before Martin popped up in the middle of his name) and you told him the story of the infamous dolls that sat prominently in the front window of your store, staring out at all that passed by on Broadway in those days, which was a bit of an eyeful by anybody's standards. You allowed that you and Jake had wanted to name your place after his song (Take me back, take me back, I want to ride in Geronimo's Cadillac) and he allowed that would have been just fine with him.

Murphey came by every time he was in town, was an avid collector of Native American art, especially E.S. Curtis gravures, and wrote a number of wonderful tunes on a beautiful Gibson Sunburst guitar he first played at your little apartment on 8th and Pearl. How that came to be is really a tale of two guitars.

There was a notorious young woman about town (we'll skip her name to protect the guilty) who had a bad habit and was inclined to steal from her friends to support it. This was clearly counter to the spirit of the times, but, then, nothing is perfect, not even at this magical time in history. She stole a pristine, pre-'60s, D-28 Martin guitar from you, the Brazilian Rosewood model with the sweetest imaginable sound, sold it for a bag of junk, and never made good on it despite all the money she eventually came into, although once more than 20 years later she mentioned in passing she was sorry for her behavior. That made two of you.

Nick the Greek, whom you had known for many a year and with whom you shared a birth-day, among other empathies, had in those days a lot of very fine guitars in his shop on Pearl Street and being the good dude that he was, he took pity on your guitarless self and sold you that Gibson for pennies on the dollar. It was great to sit around and strum that beautiful guitar, making the best of your clumsy fingers and your lack of skill, and realizing the instrument was far better than your ability to play it and always would be. Still, it sounded great.

When Murphey came by your place late one afternoon and happened to see that guitar, he asked to play it and did so for an hour or more, singing one great tune after another and playing like Johnny B. Goode gone country (just like ringing a bell). Finally, he looked at you and said, "I want this guitar and I'm going to buy it from you," and you said, "no," and he said, "I'm not leaving here until this guitar is mine." You knew he was serious and that your guitar had found a player worthy of it. So, Michael Martin Murphey bought your guitar, and wrote a number of very good songs on it, and played it in concert for many a year. Somewhere, no doubt, to this very day, the guitar gods are thankful for his intervention.

Jimmy Guercio was a customer, too. He'd show up in jeans and boots, a Western shirt with a goose down vest, and a broad-brimmed cowboy hat. Clearly, he had acclimated. Jimmy, of course, was an amazing guy. He'd played with the Beach Boys, produced Chicago, had under his hat a few dozen gold records, and in your experience, at least, he was the nicest guy in the world. He liked Navajo rugs, which you had by the dozens, and blankets, which were rarer. The subject of your conversations often turned to Caribou Ranch, which he was in the throes of turning into a world-renowned recording studio and destination for the biggest acts in rock & roll. Part and parcel was his interest in a certain rug that hung in the back room of your gallery.

Twenty-Seven Birds in a Cornfield was a pictorial weaving of exactly that. It was a 10x12 feet in size, a gray field with green corn stalks on which sat 27 birds of various postures and colors, all framed by a perfectly woven geometric border in black and white. It was made by famed weaver Alice Yellowhair, a Navajo by then in late middle age, and an unknown apprentice who helped her create the piece over two and a half years of constant work on a loom made of very large cottonwood branches they built by hand. What is 5 years of fine weaving worth? You and Jimmy discussed that subject over several years.

The time inevitably comes when a person as able as Jim Guercio has the money a person as desperate as you needs to meet the demands of another day. "Jimmy," you said, when you reached him by phone, "we may be ready to consummate that deal." You told him the price. He agreed, and said, "Why don't you and Jake come to dinner tonight? Bring that beautiful rug and I'll have a check ready for you."

You made the drive up Boulder Canyon and over to Caribou Ranch, where the two of you joined Jimmy and a whole lot of high priced talent in sharing a wonderful meal, a lot of laughs, and the handing over, finally, of an absolutely exquisite, one of a kind work of art. It was the last time you ever saw it, although you believe it hung in a place of honor at that extraordinary piece of rock & roll heaven, and you've always believed, too, it somehow survived the fire that one day in 1985 destroyed the studio.

According to reputation, some 150 different artists recorded their work at Caribou, including stalwarts as diverse as Chick Corea, Carole King, U2, War, Elton John, Stevie Wonder, John Denver, Rod Stewart, Phil Collins, Billy Joel, Steely Dan, Dennis Wilson, Al Di Meola, George Duke, Michael Jackson, Jeff Beck, the Beach Boys, and Jerry Lee Lewis, just to name a very mixed handful. Not to mention one John Lennon.

Caribou Studios, like most of the traditional parts of the recording industry, prospered during the golden age and eventually faded away. Jimmy and his crew had a profound impact not only on the business but on the place Colorado came to hold in the imagination of the music business and the musicians who made it happen. There were lots of places you could cut a few tunes, from one coast to the other, in the Caribbean and over seas, but many musicians with the clout to get their wish had a very good time making music at 8,000 feet in the Rockies.

Celebrities of every sort passed through your gallery over time. The most famous of all, especially in your heart, was Tita Morris, later Lucretia Weems, whom you first met there and who one day many years later would become your wife. There were many other famous and nearly famous folks who visited.

Writers like William Burroughs, Allen Ginsberg, and Anne Waldman; politicians like Dick and Dottie Lamm, Josie and Rollie Heath, and Bob Nelson, the attorney general of Wyoming, who took one look around and hired you to buy him one of the largest collections available at that time so he could start a gallery of his own; the mayor and all the city council at one time or another, and all the Boulder County commissioners; the famous marathoner Frank Shorter, who made it a regular stop on his daily run to down a few cups of artesian well water from the Deep Rock dispenser in the office; the astronaut Scott Carpenter, one of the Mercury Seven, who flaunted the right stuff; Monique St. Pierre, the yowsa Lange ski boot model who was 1977 Playmate of the Year; and, even Lolita herself, Sue Lyon, who was dating an inmate at Canõn City; so many artists known and unknown of every imaginable discipline; lots of musicians from every level of fame and success who were passing through town or maybe were in residence; lots of people from the University, especially the noted authority on Navajo weaving, Joe Ben Wheat, and many museum curators like Royal Hassrick, Richard Conn, and Frederick Docksteader; dealers in art and antiques from every corner of the country; lots and lots of foreigners, especially Europeans and Asians,

Warm Inside

all of whom seemed especially attuned to the importance of the art; John Echo Hawk of that well known and accomplished family, who founded the Native American Rights Fund up the street on Broadway; and many Native American people from all over the West and the Southwest, including some of them selling, a few of them buying, and most of them like everyone else who passed through the door, just there to look and feel and absorb the beauty. Then, too, there was a holy man.

One day, in fact, when you were perched high on a pretty rickety ladder, an apt metaphor for the business you were conducting, which was brilliant and soulful, educational, of a very keen aesthetic and, for most of its existence, was hanging by a thread; and you were there in the gallery on that ladder hanging a rug way up on the wall, when the gentle tinkle of the bell that rang whenever someone entered softly tolled and you looked back over your shoulder from where the ladder now was wavering 10 degrees at least back and forth in both directions and saw a small coterie of saffron-robed monks coming through the big brass door.

They were followed by a very impressive figure, much more elaborately and elegantly robed, for whom the monks held the door and bowed their heads as he entered. He was obviously Tibetan, a Buddhist monk of very high rank and appropriate gravitas, who entered the gallery, looked around the room with astute curiosity, finally to raise his eyes to where you waved like a flag in an uncertain breeze. You looked at him and he looked at you, and slowly enough a broad smile creased his face as he accepted your predicament.

Karmapa Rimpoche was said to be the 3rd highest ranking official in the Gelug School of Tibetan Buddhism. He was in Boulder to bring the blessing of His Holiness the Dalai Lama, the 14th incarnation of the Buddha Gautama, to the founding of the Naropa Institute. One of the blessings was his performance of the sacred Black Hat ceremony, something never before done outside the East.

This great teacher spent a fair amount of time examining the tribal art your gallery displayed, and once you made it safely down the ladder you were able to escort his entourage from place to place, painting to painting, basketry to pottery, weavings and jewelry, and on to pieces of parchment, quillwork and beadwork. He looked carefully at many of the various works of art, and though his English-speaking interpreters asked about the uses of this piece, the meanings of the symbols on that piece, and you were struck by the depth of his curiosity and the intimacy that developed in your efforts to answer his very astute questions.

There was a lot of beautiful and important material in your gallery, and this holy man seemed to appreciate it deeply in a way that it deserved. As the tour was completed, he looped back to certain pieces and his focus came to rest most intently on the works of the Hopi, who may be the oldest of all the indigenous peoples of North America. In fact, your gallery was named Oraivi, the original spelling of the Third Mesa home of the Hopi people. It means Rock on High.

You communicated all you knew about these people, who dwell in ancient settlements on three high mesas in Arizona, and who have highly evolved, very complex religious and social ceremonies, and who physically look like very close relatives of this entourage of Buddhist monks with whom you are conversing.

After a time, Karmapa Rinpoche and his escorts left, just after he looked at you, smiled, and nodded what you took to be thanks. People from Naropa who followed up with you said that this holy man left Boulder after his time here and travelled to the Third Mesa at Hopi, where he and the elders of the tribe conferred privately and later publicly conducted a sacred rain ceremony in the depths of a persistent draught, and that then it rained for four straight days.

You have come to believe over time that anything is possible and most of the more fantastic things are improbable. But you always loved this story and cherished the moment it began for you when they walked through the door and into your life. What you loved even more was the rest of the story you were told, which is that any person upon whom Karmapa looks is blessed for life. So be it. That part really works for you. Been counting on it, in fact.

Barricades and the first few umbrellas harken the beginning of the end. / credit:Carnegie Library for Local History

23

MALLED

THIS WAS WELL BEFORE ESCOFFIER took hold of the restaurant trade, here, there, and everywhere, and not too far ahead of the time when old Boulder came to a painful halt and new Boulder was birthed. The vivid demarcation line was the Mall. I was malled in Boulder. So were you. All good things, as they say...

When Valentine's Hardware left its longtime location at the corner of Broadway and Pearl, the long steep slide to yuppiedom began. What had been a small town of immense charm, everything you wanted to do within easy walking distance or a five minute ride on your bike, people who ranged in age and style and color and competence, and especially in wealth or lack thereof, a place of extraordinary beauty that was tolerant, livable and actually affordable, became too quickly an exorbitant playground for trust-funders and their minions. In short order, it was haute cuisine, boutiques, manses and mini-manses, and a city that sadly turned into the largest shopping mall in America. Wall to wall commerce for the hip and well-heeled. Unaffordable for the rest.

Fortunately, there was a lot of the old spirit still to be had, many wonderful things to experience, a lot of very soulful people in residence who cared more about relating than acquisitions. We are family, Sly told us, and so many of us continued to believe, even as the cracks appeared in the path we walked and the first faint notes of the swan song began.

You can't go home again, we're told. A time and a season. All of those ways of reminding ourselves that life moves on, everything changes for better or worse, and there is no purpose in lamenting what passes away. For a while, it is your time, your age, your oyster, and then it's not. So it was in Boulder. There's every good reason, though, to recall that very special time and place before it is irredeemably forgotten and vanishes in the vapors.

The Real KFML AM & FM staff and friends, 1972

24

TURN YOUR RADIO ON

R ADIO, ONCE AGAIN, WAS A HUGE FACTOR in the music scene. Unlike the days of Top 40, though, the power structure had shifted. There were three principal things that changed: the prominence of the singer/songwriter; the emergence of the record album, rather than 45 rpm singles, as the format for delivering their music; and, the emergence of stereophonic FM radio, rather than monaural AM, as the vehicle for broadcasting it to an avid fan base. There was a very healthy, symbiotic relationship among the musicians, the promoters, the record labels, the radio stations, and the audience, each of them feeding the others, and being fed.

Free-form radio, the anti-format approach to serving that public, was an idea whose time had come. Unfortunately, it also went very quickly. Commerce prefers the predictable. Corporate media interests were no less appalled than the rest of the establishment by all these freaks who arrived on the scene and the free-form way they approached their lives. So, much as they were tempted for a time to see what profit could be made from it, they pretty quickly reverted to form. Control was the issue. Free-form, by definition, was not controllable. Hence, its days were numbered almost as soon as it began. But it was glorious, if brief. At that intersection where those three changes met, free-form radio was the perfect medium to deliver the message.

Due to amended regulations in the late Sixties, the FM band came to be carried on all radios that were produced thereafter. These low wattage stations, born of high-fidelity and stereophonics, previously the scene of very parochial interests and often the creation of hobbyists broadcasting on 5 watt transmitters, came to play a significant role in the dissemination of the new culture. There was a moment when even in the biggest cities and especially the modest enclaves where people increasingly chose to dwell, it was truly community radio.

The first of all the free-form radio players in Denver, Brian Kreizenbeck, began by doing late nights at KFML-FM in 1968, a short-lived, groundbreaking effort, which would have another, much bigger and longer-lived iteration in just a few years. Kreizenbeck, the Super Warthog, did that first free-form radio show, after agreeing with the station owner, Tim O'Connor, who additionally was a promoter of boxing matches, that they would split the advertising revenues Brian generated selling spots he produced himself for a small but growing group of hipster shopkeepers around town plugging their wares on his nightly show. The arrangement worked great until the revenues began to approach $5,000 monthly, at which time their handshake agreement metastasized into a sickly $100 salary per week for the talent and not so honorable O'Connor kept the rest.

Brian's demise, a model for free-form radio prelude, performance, and aftermath that would play out repeatedly at different stations for different staff all over the country, came from a public service spot he reproduced. It was a basic recruitment ad for the Denver Police Department, which Brian sent out over the public airways verbatim, except for an overdub of hysterical laughter he added to the background. The powers that be were not amused. Brian was sent packing. But it wasn't the last we'd hear of him or free-form radio at KFML.

Radio artistry enjoyed a few fitful spasms of life at one FM station and another after Kreizenbeck set and then left the stage. Max Floyd, a top 40 jock for most of his career who had a notable moment at KLZ-FM, where the staff played album cuts instead of 45s (extended cut of "Inna-godda-da-vida," anyone?), raising a chimera of free-form radio in the corporate domain that actually was tightly programmed by Max himself, a future inductee into the Rock & Roll Hall of Fame, perhaps for the modicum of daring he exhibited in the day.

A trio of odd fellows at KMYR-FM, two of whom, Craig Bowers and Art Robertson, had recently sold the station to mighty Doubleday Broadcasting but stayed on as hired help, and another guy, Ed Mitchell aka Ed Hepp (for real), who'd been a big deal in radio out west, took a flyer on free-form radio. Art was also the station's engineer, the quintessential Mr. Jones noting that something was happening here but not what it was, only that he suddenly was surrounded by a rising tide of antisocial commie creeps that threatened to swamp his boat.

They hired four even odder characters, being Steve Burke (he of the very deep and mellifluous voice, who would caress the airwaves for years thereafter, from one venue or another); Thom Trunnell, another deep-voiced and deeply committed aficionado of creative radio, who would have a long and determined,

Thom Trunnell gunning down another radio banality, near Boulder, CO 1972

if somewhat checkered, career on Denver airwaves; young Randy Morrison, who racked up impressive ratings in his late night slot, sufficient to give the suits some hope this motley crew might bring them success, a dream that evaporated rather quickly when the scope of what they had unleashed became apparent; and, Bill Ashford, a legend in his own time and mind, who was perhaps the ultimate free-form radio personality, for better or worse, and all that entailed.

In short order, thanks to happenstance, Trunnell was program director and Herb Neu was Sales Manager. It was a fortuitous moment in free-form history, not long to last but vital because of the relationships that formed, the strong sense of the possibilities it suggested, and the credentials it conveyed.

In less than a year, they'd all been sent packing when the wary suits at Doubleday suddenly came to their senses. The station would go its merry and mostly mainstream way, having like a gyroscope righted itself to the mediocre mean, and soon enough would become KHOW-FM, home of Hal & Charley and others of the audio enemas broadcast each day that were cathartic efforts to deal with life in increasingly restless urban America.

Fits and starts. Where corporate radio in 1970 flirted with going, like an adolescent's wet dream that in the middle of the night was a screaming passion but in the light of morning little more than a mess, some very small entities just did it. There was a gang at KCFR-FM, the little station at DU with a signal strength that covered the campus and maybe a few blocks beyond, here and there, was doing some interesting stuff. Jim Sprinkle, who was a very young guy back then, was one of the team whose name you recall, mainly because he continued over the years to do free-form radio and, later, concert promotion with an unforgettable voice and remarkably deft style. KCFR hung in there for many a year thereafter, growing in signal strength and influence even as the corporate competition ebbed and flowed. Much ebb, rare flow.

A man named Joe McGoey sold a soft drink bottling company and bought a radio station. Bought it from Tim O'Connor, in fact. What to do with it? No doubt a lot of different ideas came and went. But one day he was approached by Brian Kreizenbeck, who talked about the potential with him, and later returned with one Thom Trunnell, a renegade Mormon from Houston by way of Salt Lake City, who looked more than a little bit suspicious but knew the lingua franca of radio programming, and a relatively sane seeming young man named Herb Neu, who knew from salesmanship and had some cred in the radio world. Joe was intrigued. Enticed, even. There actually appeared to be possibilities.

They would work cheap, build an audience among all these young kids who loved rock & roll, and when great success had been achieved, all of them, as Joe no doubt had dreamed, would cash in, sharing in the money. That was the idea, strange bedfellows be damned. Joe said, okay! Do it. Off they went.

KFML, for all that it accomplished and the iconic status it achieved in radio lore, lasted less than two years, at least in this incarnation. But what years they were! You were a small part of it and hence your bias is a factor, but you can make the case that more competence, more artistry, more innovation, more daring and dazzling and flat out, balls to the wall, go-for-it genius stuff happened in that brief moment in time at KFML-FM than has happened in all the rest of radio in Denver for all time.

The loyalty that grew from those efforts enveloped everyone except the suits. The audience and the announcers grew to be connected at the hip (so to speak); the musicians started hanging out there whenever they were in town – hell, Charlie Daniels slept on the couch three or four times on tours when he couldn't afford a motel; it wasn't long before big time artists were playing mini-concerts on the air and soon full blown live casts of their music exclusively on the station. The local promoters loved KFML, so did the A&R guys from the record labels. Movie studios by way of the local distributors came on board. Eventually, proof positive in this still crassly commercial world of radio, the sponsors, even the corporations like Ford and Pepsi, eventually blinked, giving up control of their ads to the station's production people. So when the station was hitting on all cylinders and its lights were blinking like a pin ball machine racking up a million points, its rather phenomenal promo man, one David Shepardson, and the oft-mentioned Thom Trunnell, its program manager, suggested to Barry Fey that, being the Stones were going to be in town for a show or two and had the next night off, and being as how KFML was too hip to need any further explanation, it seemed perfectly logical that the station should host a party for The Boys at Barry's Cherry Hills home. Why not?

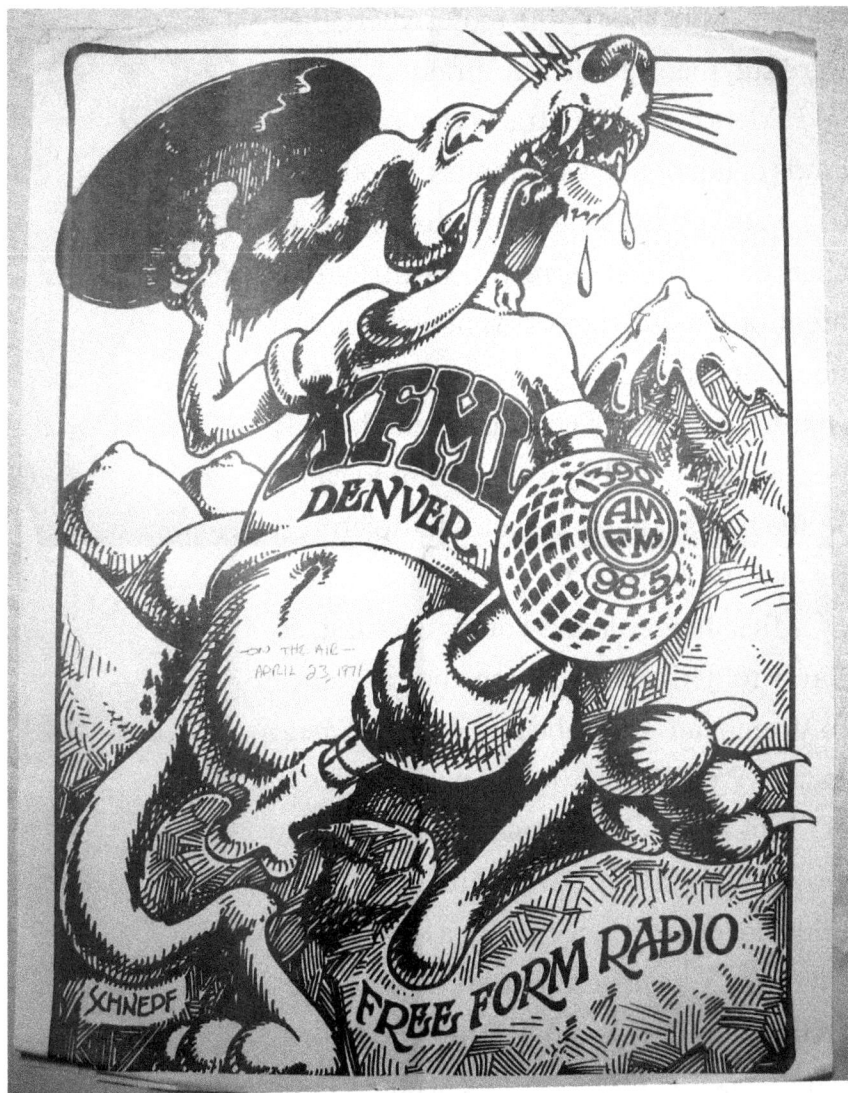

What cinched it was this. There was a photographer named Dan Fong, who like in real life pops up here and there and everywhere throughout this book. In his career, which spanned the Seventies and well beyond, he photographed just about every band that ever played Denver, Boulder, or the few other local venues where big time rock & roll held sway. He'd done a lot of other stuff, too.

Now Fong is very clever and has his ways, but still you might wonder how this guy ended up backstage at every concert, getting shots of all these famous folks hanging out and, then, all these awesome shots of those same people up on stage and deep into their thing. Here is the plain and simple truth: the way to a band's heart is through its stomach.

Dan Fong knew how to cook. When he appeared on the scene, backstage was a case of beer and potato chips. On the '69 tour in Fort Collins, when the band asked Barry Fey about food, he told the Stones to try the motel where they were staying. '72 was way different. Bands had riders to their contracts that said what kinds of liquor and what kinds of food were to be served backstage by what kinds of chefs on lavish tables resting on an assortment of Persian carpets that covered the floors of the dressing rooms. Every band that tasted Fong's cooking signed on. If he was in town, they wanted him to cater. While he was there, he took a few pictures. It was simple as that.

Mick Jagger loved Fong's cooking, so Barry told him, let's give the boy a chance to stretch out. How about a 13 course meal for 40? Well, 80 showed up, but it got done. A Chinese-Hawaiian luau that absolutely wowed everybody. Two whole roast pigs, and a lot of very tasty courses beforehand That party has been written up on Fong's website, in Barry's book, and who knows where else. It was a helluva scene. There were beautiful people in every nook and

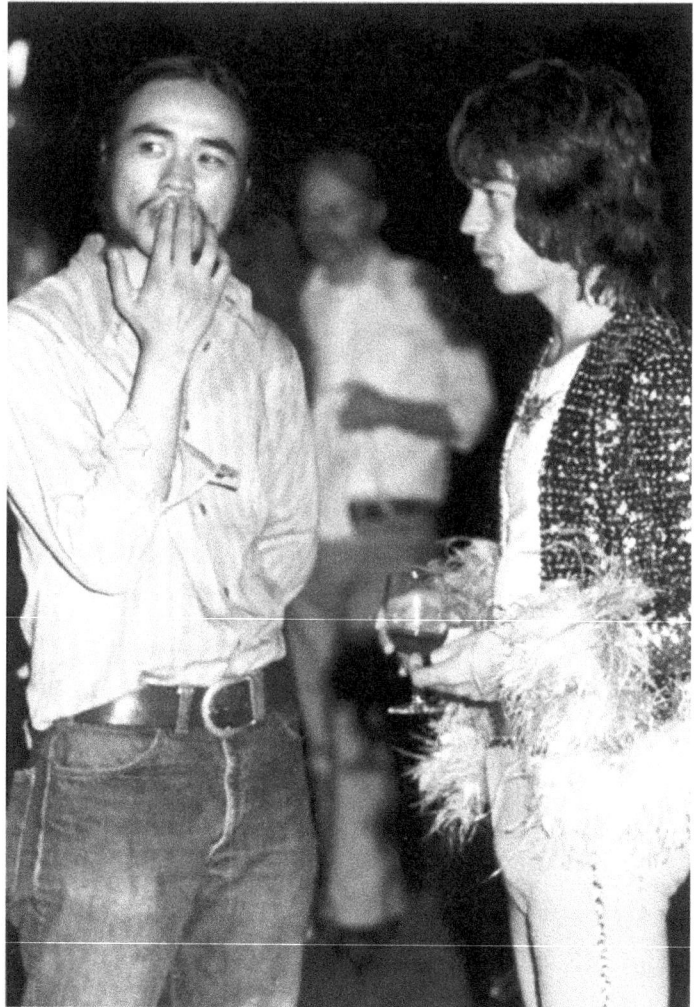

Dan Fong, Mick Jagger—Denver, CO 1972
photographer unknown

cranny of the night, food and drink and drugs and every manner of intoxication, the strongest dose of which was merely being in the presence of rock & roll royalty, having the time of your life.

In the many wrinkles of that event, between the chair-sized Styrofoam mushrooms that littered the lawn, the Rolling Stones logo that foamed at the mouth, the long, low tables covered with sumptuous food of every sort, all of the folks seated there, the waves of beautiful young women who, in addition to being hip and happening, also loved the music like the rest of us and were happy to assist Dan and his helpers to serve up this extravagant and extraordinary meal, and who somehow you couldn't help but notice spent an inordinate amount of time in their wanderings in the very near vicinity of Mick—go figure—there was maybe a dim memory reverberating through that night of the time not very long before when all of you, the Feys, the Stones, the radio people and everyone else in attendance, all of you were just kids and none of you could have imagined finding yourself in such a place as this.

Joe McGoey, Marcello Cabus, Jr., the author, Brian Kreizenbeck, Bill Wyman, Bill Ashford, Harry Tuft, Denver, CO 1972

"HOOKED"

25

OR CROOKED

S EX, DRUGS, AND ROCK & ROLL. What some day would be called branding. We've spoken at length about the rock & roll. What about the sex? Sex! That's what people really want to hear about. Right? Come on, already! Enquiring minds want to know.

There was a lot of it. You probably heard. It's true. Every bit of it. And you are glad. But you don't kiss and tell. Do you? People were trying to break free of their inhibitions in all the aspects of their lives. Sex was certainly an aspect. A very big one, in many instances.

When you spend a lot of time in close proximity, having fun, being soulful, exploring who you are and what you want, how this new life of yours might be; and, well, yeah, taking drugs and running around naked together, one thing can lead to another, you know? Stuff happens. Blissfully. You tried to be good to people and people were good to you. You were always lucky that way. Maybe you all were. 'Nuff said.

Well, maybe one short story. No names. A person previously mentioned, who was a stunning beauty, asked you if you'd take her out to celebrate her 21st birthday. Well, yeah! Okay! She wanted to go, of all places, to the Blue Parrot in Louisville, one of the cluster of Italian restaurants in that little town where families gathered for pasta and red sauce. Apparently, they had refused to serve her wine a number of times before she was of age. Now she wanted to get it done.

When you picked her up, present in hand, she came to the door in a rather spectacular dress, one open at the neck nearly to each shoulder and plunging from there past her rather ample breasts to a point somewhere south of her navel. "Wow," was about the best you could say.

The entrance she made at the restaurant left a lot of tongues hanging from the mouths of the males in the room, glasses readjusted on their noses and eyes very wide, while mothers tried frantically to distract their children. "Hey, mom, look at her!" Dad was already looking, pretty intensely, in fact. They kept right on looking, too. Many a meatball bounced into many a lap that night. Dinner was like a picnic besieged by human ants. She lapped up every minute of it, right down to the bottom of the bottle of wine.

She and you nearly died twice that night. It was a time of "ologies." All those studies. Psychology, sociology, biology, astrology, phrenology, mythology, numerology. Symbols had meaning. Everything was profound. It was all a big deal. You thought stuff meant stuff. Things mattered. It was a costly illusion. Especially this night.

So, when you took a moonlight hike in the hills after dinner, and at one point where you crested a small hill, the two of you nearly walked into a stretch of high voltage electrical line that had dipped dangerously from it's towers, it gave you pause.

When you returned to your home with her and began to roll around a bit, rather vigorously exploring each other, the second incident occurred. A fellow you knew sold waterbeds, newly introduced, rather primitive early versions, and this one rested on a pallet, no sides to hold it in place. It was like a horizontal queen-sized sofa in the living room, unused to this sort of activity. She and you were both big people and, passions being what they were, you were making a lot of waves.

Literally so. At a point where better things were pending, you suddenly found yourselves flying through the air, flung to the floor, and no sooner did you land than a polyvinyl tidal wave washed over you, covering you completely and, fortunately, ebbing back the other way immediately thereafter. Instinctively, you both pushed it along and it flopped back up onto the pallet from whence it came.

You laughed hysterically and eventually regained your composure, but neither of you was anxious to get back on that bed. As funny as it was, some things take on an ominous significance as you begin to fully absorb them. You're not sure what it means but surely it means something? Something to be careful of? You begin to suspect it does. Unfortunately, this was one of them. Neither of you said much about it afterwards but neither did you ever get together again.

Music has magic. No doubt a lot of romance was spawned at all these concerts, too. It was joyous to go off into the dark of night to one place and another, hear some beautiful tunes with a bunch of other people who, like you, were letting go, feeling good, looking for adventure, having at it. There was a freedom of expression both on stage and off that everyone was digging, and in the full bloom of youth, with so much energy in play, and hormones, too, there was a thick atmosphere of beauty and vivaciousness that settled on one and all. It was very appealing.

Some of the shows tilted way to that side. When Tony Funches and a guy named Butch Grayer brought Al Green to the Coliseum early in 1973, everybody fell in love. C'mon already. Hold your warm and tender body close to mine? Well, okay! For the good times, indeed. You were willing. An on-and-off fifteen year relationship kicked into gear that night with the woman who eventually birthed your son.

Dark Star, as they called themselves, did another show, this time Waylon Jennings at the Boulderado Hotel, that was a sun-drenched, drug-addled blast. Every room at the hotel that faced the courtyard where Jennings played became a party unto itself, each corridor a hall of mirrors and every door a portal to the next scene in line (and lines). The Outlaw put on a helluva show, and all the baby outlaws drank and smoked and snorted and who knows what all to their hearts' content. Don't know why but it was last show Dark Star ever did.

Maybe we can talk about drugs? This might be the place to do it. We're talking, after all, sex, drugs, and rock & roll. All of it unprecedented. At least in such volume, with such celebration. This wasn't quiet. It wasn't demure. It was pretty much in your face.

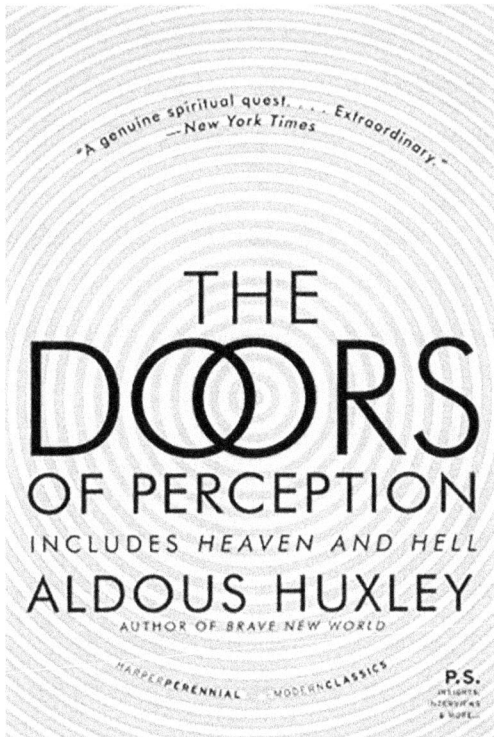

Whether you were willing or not, it was rather hard to ignore. You've heard the saying, "Don't trust anyone over 30." That was a way of distinguishing this generation from the others. What you may not know is that there was a widely held belief you should not trust anyone who hadn't done LSD. Yet.

That was thought to be evidence of just how far gone your generation was, but there was a belief in the ability of psychedelics to undo the ego and open up the pathways to a more spiritual perspective; to provide a big picture look at the individual in the scope of all nature and the cosmos; and, to reconnect the person to the entire organism of life.

The scorn the establishment heaped on that belief, that instinct, that aspiration is finally being undone by studies of the brain and lessons being learned about how psychedelics do exactly that: deconstruct the ego and offer you a vision of yourself as part of a deeply interconnected whole. Under their influence, there is no me, there is only we. The ego is dissolved and the effects appear to last for a considerable period of time. There is a serenity.

Psychedelic therapy, in fact, is not only the au courant movement in mental health care, it is believed by some to be the doorway to a comprehensive theory of mental illness and treatment. From the mouths of babes, it seems.

When you realize that all the garbage Big Pharma has pumped into your system for so many years has come to absolutely nothing good, and you're still as over-amped and undermotivated as before, and everybody that you know is still exactly as crazy as they've always been, the shrink may suggest you spend a little time chewing on some mushrooms and letting go. Let's uncouple that ego from your view and see what there is to see. We are family! We are the same, whatever we do. Get up everybody and sing. Song of the Sixties, anyone?

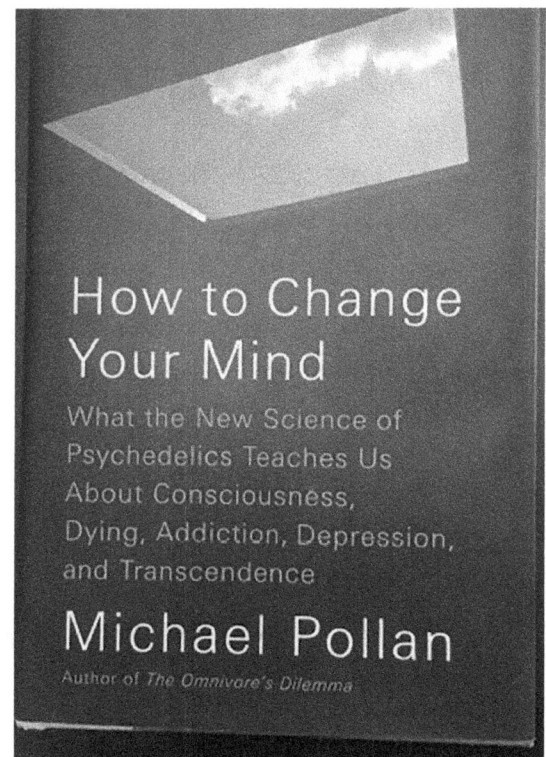

Drugs have always been around. Every society of record has indication of intoxicants, of drugs, of herbs both sacred and profane. People who study such things have all sorts of tales to tell, depending on whose ox they want to gore, which agency is funding their study, what baggage they bring to the room.

There is ample evidence for those who care to look that addiction affects some 5 to 10% of civilization, a figure that is pretty consistent over time. That's not to say that they are the only users, though, nor even the only regular users. They're just the ones who're hooked. It is their principal, if not their only, focus.

When the Stones in 1966 sang a song about Mother's Little Helper, they were on to something. Valley of the Dolls, you know. There's a story here to tell. A narrative arc: Miltown, Librium, Valium. Tranquilizers for mom. Very nice to have. Get you through the day. Blissfully. Then came ADD. Ritalin for those over-amped children who were driving you over the edge. Dope for the kids. Dope for the adults. Dope for all. Drugs for every occasion. Doctor's orders.

We think about addiction to drugs in terms of heroin users and Alcoholics Anonymous. We're sold the idea that "drugs" are different than pharmaceuticals, that "pushers" sell drugs and "doctors" dole out medicine. Drugs are proscribed, medicine is prescribed.

Marijuana, hashish, kef, peyote, psilocybin, mescaline, opium, coca, betel, alcohol, nicotine, caffeine are among the many naturally occurring psychoactive agents that have accompanied humankind through its evolution, some of them nearly from the beginning of history. All are proscribed in this country but the last three, at least one of which, nicotine, is proven deadly, and one of which, alcohol, has probably wrought more mayhem in society than all the rest combined.

Then there are the pharmaceuticals, way too numerous to name. Watch the nightly news if you want to catch the latest and the greatest: drugs for tragic maladies like Restless Leg Syndrome; or that beauty known simply as the Little Purple Pill, rising from the meadow of flowers like a butterfly to calm your every frazzled nerve; pills for your heart, stomach, liver, kidneys, bowels, sphincter, prostate, bladder, ears, nose, throat, sexual organs, your nerves themselves, and then, of course, a vast variety for your brainpan. And another vast variety for pain, everything from aspirin to opiates. All are prescribed. How many would you like today?

U.S. expenditures on prescription drugs in 2017 exceeded $360 billion, or roughly $9,000 each for every man, woman, and child. That doesn't count over the counter medicine, nor does it count all the prescription drugs that find their way into the black market, where they become proscribed.

You suspect the proscribed market is very sizable, as well. Marijuana, which has become legal in one manner or another in 25 states and Canada, is already a $multi-billion market in its legal form alone. Whatever you may think of drug consumption, and however you define what's right or wrong about it, there is clearly a whole lot of it going on. People like their dope. Okay?

It was a lot less so in the years you're discussing here. The growth in consumption per capita of drugs of every sort has grown exponentially from the post-war era to modern times. Recreational drugs have become far more widely acceptable. But it is the growth in prescription drugs that has skyrocketed. Big Pharma has done very well, indeed. Something has to sooth that rampant ego.

You think about all this and bother to write it down here because, while the Fifties and Sixties saw some evidence of what was to come, and the counterculture in the last half of the Sixties was thought to be thoroughly saturated with psychedelics and marijuana, it wasn't until the Seventies that drugs became such a pungent social force with so little anymore to recommend them. The problems began to exceed the pleasure. You might wonder why.

There was a time when enterprising young people who were looking for adventure would travel to Michoacan, Guerrero, or Oaxaca with a duffel bag full of Levis, which back then could only be bought Stateside, and trade them for a few pounds of marijuana, which they then would put into that same duffel bag and bring them home to their friends. That was hippie trade. Low risk, low profit, lots of fun.

It became a lot more business-like when the risk increased. If you make it harder to get, the price goes up, the profit margin gets bigger, and a different sort of player gets involved. And when profit becomes the principal if not the only motive, efficiency dictates that some drugs make a better business than others.

Scale, volume, ROI, you know? Those sorts of calculations that can drive business to greater success. Why haul a plane load of pot when you can realize a hundred times the profit with a plane load of cocaine? Same risk, much greater reward. Duh! And, hey, everybody can use a little bump now and again. You dig?

Bump, unfortunately, is what was happening everywhere with increasing frequency as the Seventies began to evolve. Cocaine entered the scene. Bam! Imperceptibly at first but soon enough with blazing clarity, a shift in the focus and momentum of this vast social experiment in counterculture living was upon us.

What was always a sense of brotherhood and community, the "we" of the tribe, increasingly became the "me" of the person with a nose full of blow, who couldn't stop talking, pacing, twitching, self-absorbing, and who thought it was perfectly okay as long as it was certain that another line or two was at hand. Maybe you were one of them.

Coke, of course, had been around for a long time. It was a favorite of the obsessive sleuth, Sherlock Holmes, and was perhaps what put some of the roar in the Roaring Twenties, perhaps even what helped kill off that notorious decade. The song, "Cocaine," was part of the standard repertoire of every folksinger in the day (running all 'round my brain). But when it insinuated itself into the daily lifestyle of the Seventies, it was a signal change in the mentality, the sociability, the vibe of the counterculture. Like Ernest Hemingway said about bankruptcy, it happened very slowly, then very suddenly. Before the decade was out, it became the focus, the terrible momentum. Casey Jones you better watch your speed.

Along the way from there to here, people snorted entire businesses, banks, brokerages, law firms, dental practices, consulting companies, many a small shop, grocery stores, tire stores, kitchen stores, service stations, radio stations, way stations, record companies, management firms, restaurants and bars, discos and strip joints, psychiatric practices and counseling services, all of them

Nose Candy

vacuumed up the nose. And many, many, many a rock & roll band, too. The Deviated Septum. Can you believe it? Maybe you were there.

There was a time in the Seventies when everywhere you went, each and every conversation began with one of two questions: Got a line? or, Want a line? There was nothing else to say. Until you did a line or two. Then, you couldn't shut up, even if no one was listening.

Your doctor was hammered, your lawyer was hammered, your banker and CPA were hammered, your broker was hammered, the guy who changes your oil was hammered; the bartender shook so bad he spilled your martini every time, the waiter nearly knocked over the table merely wiping it off, and the cook was out back in the alley snorting and smoking while the pasta turned to mush; your wife, your girlfriend, your friends, your enemies, all of them were looking for the next line. For a while, it seemed pretty normal. Just part of the scene.

We all have our Jones, it seems. Whether yours was gathered and fed legally or whether you played on the black market was the issue at hand. Big Pharma and it's lackeys in the health care industry, the pharmaceutical delivery system, were on a roll. That was just business reaping ever greater rewards. No reason for caution there.

The War on Drugs, of course, was focused on the illicit users, and virtually no stoner was left unturned. The trillions of dollars lavishly spent in that cynical and calculated exercise showed many an accomplishment: the dramatic growth of the prison industry, a per capita rate of incarceration that vastly exceeds any other nation in the world, and the incentivising of vigorous criminal enterprises here, in Mexico, and South America. Not to mention the poppy fields of Asia.

Over time, it succeeded in creating a terrorist nation on our southern border. And more of them further south. It funded political suppression and political insurrection at different times in different places. It underwrote nearly every urban police department in the U.S., supplied them with surplus military hardware, and turned them into inner-city combat units. It even subsidized the C.I.A. and put the air beneath the wings of Flying Tiger Airlines. It had many uses in many different places where the government wanted to apply some pressure.

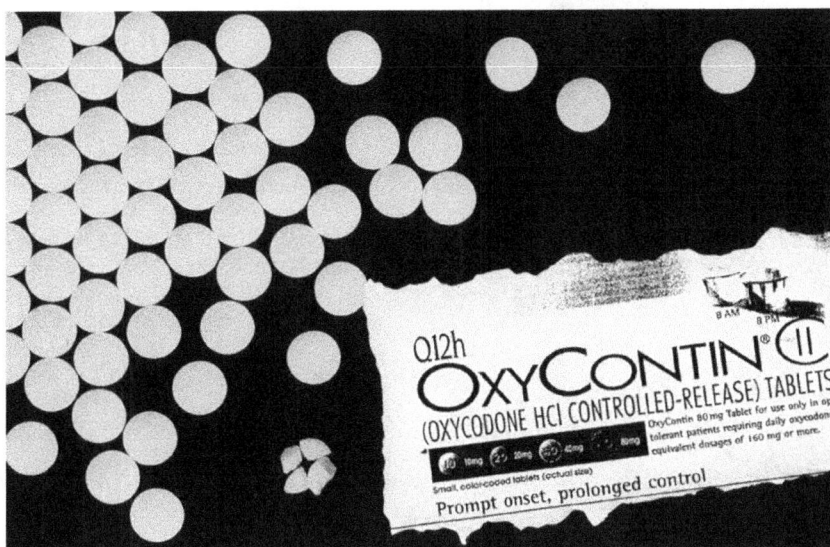

What it didn't do is stop the flow of drugs. From legal or illegal sources. They just kept coming. Maybe that was the idea, when all was said and done. Religion was no longer the opiate of the masses. Opiates were the opiate of the masses. Commerce was reason enough. And the rivers of dollars flowed.

26

BOOKED

BARRY FEY REPUTEDLY SOLD MORE CONCERT TICKETS than any promoter in rock & roll history. Make that any "independent" promoter. Rock & roll has gone on to concert promotion of a scale that was inconceivable back when, thoroughly corporate in its outcome like most everything else that was incubated in the day.

Barry was the first and last of his kind, the guy who did it one screaming, profanity-laced phone call at a time, one band at a time, one agent at a time, in competition with all the other guys just like him who were trying to make a buck putting on shows that kids wanted to see and hear. They invented the concert promotion business out of whole cloth. Fey may have been the best of them all.

There were promoters in Denver before he arrived, like Ed Weimer, Hugh Hooks, and Robert Garner, but that's not the type of guys we're talking about. They were old school. Once he got rolling, Fey blew them all away.

Like most everything else in America, it was a time when independence and independents showed us the way, just before the corporate birds of prey swooped in from on high, seeing everything below them that was making money as potential carrion they'd eventually feast on like road kill. Guys like Barry Fey, and there were precious few of them, created a business that filled a need. For a time, and whatever its faults, it was uncharted, unrestricted, entrepreneurial, and glorious.

He already had put on a lot of shows, every one of them successful, if not without their problems. Off the top of his head, Fey could tell you the who, what, where, why, when, naming the date, band, venue, tickets sold, gross and net for each of them without batting an eye. He had an amazing mind for details, but even more impressive was his instinct for what would sell. He sold out every single show for many years, never was rained out when they were held outside, never had a cancellation or had to give a refund.

The list of his accomplishments is staggering. He brought the Family Dog to Denver; booked Mammoth Gardens for Stu Green; single-handedly did the Denver Pop Festival in 1969; kickstarted stadium shows by booking the first show on the first tour of that type when the Stones played Fort Collins in 1969; partnered with Chuck Morris to revitalize the small club scene with Ebbets Field downtown and later the Rainbow Music Hall in Southeast Denver; brought recognition to Red Rocks as the finest outdoor venue in the world by staging the Summer of Stars there for many years; and, not incidentally being a partner in the production and filming of Under the Blood Red Sky, which U2 performed in perhaps the most hellacious conditions of any concert ever held there, and which Rolling Stone magazine later called one of the 50 greatest moments in rock & roll history. If there was a band or a fan anywhere who hadn't heard of Red Rocks before then, they had now.

That was Barry Fey. In his spare time, he created Old Timers Baseball at Mile High and made it a Father's Day tradition; sold 20,000 tickets to a flag football game between John Elway's team of used-to-bes and one led by Joe Montana; and, in his spare time, managed to rescue the Denver Symphony Orchestra from bankruptcy as one sorely mismanaged organization.

That, and managing to gamble away a small fortune on horse races and football games. In an age of rampant drinking and drug use, Fey was having none of it. Never touched the stuff, except as a lark. But gambling was his Jones. Food and gambling. Food nearly killed him when he reached almost 400 pounds and could barely walk from his office at 16th and Champa across the street to the Woolworth's lunch counter. But he survived that. Got his act together, maybe his stomach stapled or whatever, but somehow he took the weight off and returned to something like normal size.

Gambling was another matter. There was no way to staple that closed. Like addicts everywhere of every sort, he spent a lot of time and effort telling you how good he was at it, how he made money gambling, what a noted handicapper he was. Maybe. Maybe not. He made millions and died broke. What to say?

That run of his from 1967 or so through the Seventies and well beyond brought nearly every big name band in rock & roll to town. It would be a shorter list by far to name the bands Barry didn't bring here. Suffice it to say that Denver, Colorado was known throughout the industry by agents, musicians, and other promoters as a first class stop on anybody's tour, and it was because Barry Fey made it so.

He wasn't very likable, he wasn't a friend, he wasn't somebody you were glad to hear from at 3 o'clock in the morning, when more than

Tommy Bolin and Chuck Morris

once he called "just to talk, Jimmy." When all was said and done, though, he was in his own strange way one of the most remarkable people you ever met. And, in his field, one of the very most accomplished. RIP, Barry Fey.

He also raised up a few associates, most notable among them Chuck Morris, who made his own mark early and often in the local music scene, and became eventually a very big part of the concert business machine that made independent promoters like Barry Fey obsolete and unemployed. Morris today runs AEC, one of the two corporations that dominate the concert business in America, and which promotes in his Western Region alone a mere 1200 concerts annually, 3.3 per day. It is staggering to contemplate.

Chuck arrived on the scene earlier than Fey and stayed longer. He was a bartender at the Sink in Boulder in the mid Sixties, talked owner Herbie Kauvar into purchasing Tulagi's when that venerable nightclub finally bellied up a few years later, and turned it into one of the hottest small venues in the country.

The list of acts that played for Morris at the Tule is too long to recite, but you were fortunate to see many of them and they included everybody who was anybody in the ranks just below the stadium acts. Bonnie Raitt made everybody's list of favorites, Dan Hicks, ZZ Top, John Lee Hooker, later on some guys from L.A. called the Eagles. In your personal pantheon of memories were these two stories about Linda Ronstadt and Muddy Waters.

Ronstadt had achieved a modicum of fame as lead singer for the Stone Ponies, and for being in those rampantly sexist days of yore a very attractive young woman. When she played Tulagi's for a couple of nights, in her time before Pirates of Penzance when she really learned to sing, she was no less lovely than advertised but her repertoire had shifted to Motown tunes, which she did less than well by.

You said so in your review that ran the next day in the paper, something about how Martha and the Vandellas were probably already spinning in the graves they one day would inhabit. When you dropped by later that day for the interview that was scheduled, her radiant face appeared when the door opened and you were struck by how beautiful she was, but only briefly. When she realized who you were, her face dissolved into an angry scowl, her head shook side to side for just a moment, and then she slammed the door in your face. No interview tonight.

Muddy Waters was an idol. You loved the blues from the time you first heard them and he was one of the giants in that field. It was really exciting to have the chance to talk with him and you wanted to be especially professional in conducting your interview. Showing respect for a truly great bluesman.

He welcomed you to the dressing room, where he and the band were relaxing. Can't remember who was playing with him those days, but you want to believe Pinetop Perkins was there. Maybe a couple of others you'd listened to on record for so many years. All these older gentlemen, dressed in suits with their ties loosened, taking a moment to nod "hello" and back to playing cards, smoking cigarettes and cooling out before the gig, while you in your embroidered shirt, bell bottoms, boots, sat down with the great Muddy Waters.

"Mr. Morganfield," you asked him, plunging ahead, "how do you feel about the resurgence of interest in the blues these days?" He looked at you from under a heavy brow and a very slight smile creased his large, meaty face. "Son," he said, "I've played nearly 300 gigs a year for the last 30 years. Don't mean shit to me."

Chuck Morris made a great local club a great national club, and when he was done with that, he and Barry Fey cut a deal to open Ebbets Field in Denver.

Being a Brooklyn boy, Chuck had a soft spot in his heart for the days when the Dodgers graced his neighborhood; hence, the name. It was housed on the main floor in a high rise downtown at 1020 15th Street, and no one will claim it was the most attractive place they ever spent an evening. The floor and walls were covered with shag carpeting, and one might have wondered about the décor, but Chuck Morris was a very smart guy and he had his reasons.

Ebbets Field held slightly fewer than 250 people in a room arranged like a ballpark where the stage was at home plate and the risers where people sat were the stands. A local company called Listen Up did the sound and it was exquisite. The room was intimate, the sound was perfect, and many a band recorded live albums there in that illustrious period of the mid-seventies. Shag carpeting helped to make it so.

The lineup of talent that passed through that club was really astounding, another part of creating the specific gravity that made Colorado a center of the music universe. You saw maybe two dozen shows there in a mere three years or so, and many are lost in the ethers. But there were performers you remember so well like the great

Dr. John, Rahsaan Roland Kirk, Asleep at the Wheel, Katy Moffat, Little Feat, Maria Muldaur, Al Kooper, Willie Nelson, Bob Seger, Pure Prairie League, Leo Kottke, Gene Clark, Stanley Clarke, Sandy Denny, Tom Waits, Ry Cooder, Fairport Convention, Chris Hillman, Freddie King, J.D. Souther, Return to Forever, and so many more it boggles the mind. Chuck in fact one day recently read to you his personal list of some 400 acts he booked there.

To see so many great performers in an intimate setting with perfect sound was an experience to cherish. You felt like you and all the rest of the audience crawled into a cocoon with the chrysalis and all of you there were about to be butterflies flitting away into the night. Maybe it was the drugs.

Ebbets Field began a resurgence of the club scene in Denver, which compared to Boulder had been lagging. There were others, like the Shapes on East Colfax, run by longtime Feyline associate Nate Feld, where many a great band played, from Savoy Brown, Energy, Baby Huey and the Babysitters, to the awesome Freddi-Henchi Band. Others, too, like the Café York, a low key, persistent venue for good shows, and the club whose name you can't remember in the building on Colfax and Holly or thereabouts where you, Harry Tuft, and Bill Ashford one evening in the early Seventies drank champagne and ate lobster tails while Lightnin' Hopkins sat on a stool a few feet away and played his particularly fierce blues, looking at you every now and then to say, "Watch the fingers, boy!" as he ran off another dazzling riff.

But, good as those club gigs were, it was the stadium shows that defined the music business for the rest of that decade and well beyond. So many great performances were visited on Colorado, in one venue or another, you would need a very lengthy appendix to list them all.

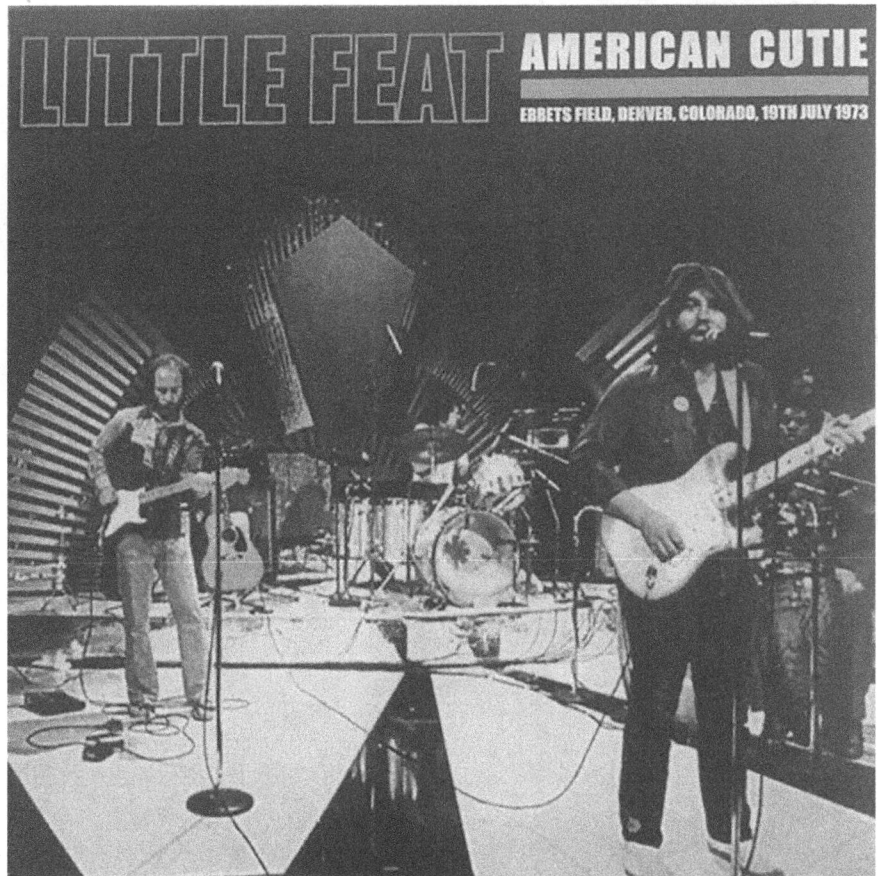

27

SEVENTIES BIG

YOU AND SO MANY OF THE PEOPLE you knew had been wrestling with big issues for years now, the chaos of the '60s, the counterculture you represented, the belief in a better way to live together, big fears, big dreams. Maybe that's why big events became such a fixation. Maybe like another walk on the moon.

We all were connected in a way that made distance far less relevant. Technology continued its relentless advance, telegraph, telephone, radio, television, all of it bringing us into more immediate interaction with everybody else. We saw things and heard things first hand we only used to hear about from others, read about, maybe dream about. Like riots, war, assassinations, mayhem of every sort.

Now they were right in front of us, no matter how far away. War on the nightly news. Look at that Napalm! Ain't that sumpin'? Tricky Dicky says he is not a crook. You heard him say so yourself. The Drug Enforcement Administration broke up the largest cartel in the entire history of the world, seizing cocaine worth a bazillion bucks and arresting most of Cartegena, Columbia tonight. Tomorrow they will break up a bigger one. Maybe it's all more than you can believe.

Your community was big. Your sense of what went on was big. Everything was big. That oft-cited web of life in which all things were connected – and whatever you do to the web, you do to yourself – was becoming very apparent.

Bob Pennetta said to you once when you were barely teenagers and wondering why everybody acted so weird, why we're all so busy posturing, that "We all think we're on television." What hath Ricky Nelson wrought? This was way, way, way before selfies. Way before social media made each of us our own little broadcast network. But it had the ring of truth. Everything was a big deal. Maybe you liked it that way.

It was a decade in Colorado neatly bisected by territorial and astrological events, by unprecedented achievements in sport, including an event that gave feminism a major shot in the arm, by a few ups and downs in your personal life, and every bit of it accompanied by a brilliant and compelling soundtrack. Music was reaching the apex of a long, successful narrative arc in rock & roll, which would be captured and sustained in style if not creative substance for many years to come. Still, the decade of the Seventies was not to be equaled again.

When Helen Reddy sang "I Am Woman (Hear Me Roar)" in 1971, it quickly became an anthem for the Women's Movement, which had moved on from burning bras to more substantial, if less foundational, matters. Feminism was playing out in debates of every sort, but it came to a very visual place when tennis bum Bobby Riggs, a 55 year old former Wimbledon winner, said women's tennis was inferior and issued a challenge to Billie Jean King for a head to head match, which she refused. He then challenged reigning champion Margaret Court, who agreed. They met on Mother's Day, May 13, 1973 in front of 5,000 fans in Ramona, California. Riggs cleaned her clock, 6-2, 6-1.

The story made the cover of Time Magazine and Sports Illustrated. Riggs once again was a celebrity. He used the spotlight to demean women's tennis and challenge one and all to prove him wrong. "I can beat any of them," he said.

Now King had to respond. She accepted an offer to meet Riggs on September 30th in the Houston Astrodome on national television in a winner-take-all, $100,000 match. It became a study in how quickly commercialism can piggyback on any event, no matter the subject, and profit from the spectacle. The Battle of the Sexes, as it was called, was fully engaged.

King came to the court held aloft on a feathered pallet carried by an entourage of handsome, barechested body builders of the male persuasion, and Riggs followed in a carriage pulled by nearly nude women of a very comely sort. They exchanged gifts, hers a piglet for the chauvinist, his a giant Sugar Daddy sucker for the little lady. The match was on.

In what may still be the largest crowd ever to watch a tennis match, both in person and on television, more than 30 thousand people in the stands, 50 million on their television sets in the U.S., and perhaps that many again worldwide, joined you and your 9 year old eldest daughter in seeing King win in straight sets, 6-4, 6-3, 6-3. Women roared, your daughter, Kate, yelled herself horse, and nothing in all the many things you read or heard over the years on the subject of women's empowerment taught you more than watching the look on your daughter's face as King ran Riggs into the ground and won the match.

In 1973, the greatest race horse of all time, Secretariat, became the first Triple Crown winner in 25 years, setting all-time track records in all three races, including a 31 length victory in the Belmont Stakes, which many call the greatest performance by a race horse ever. There have been only 13 Triple Crown winners in racing history; for whatever reason, they come in clusters with long stretches of failed attempts in between. The 1940s was the most prolific decade with four; the 1970s would see three, including back to back winners in 1977 and '78. Those two, Seattle Slew and Affirmed, are the only two Triple Crown winners that eventually raced each other, with Slew winning both. Last year Justify joined the ranks.

In terms of music that makes the pulse race, you've heard your share. But, the Call to the Post at the race track with its bugle burst of eighth notes in the ascending passages is in a class by itself, summoning these powerful horses to the gate for the moment they were born and bred to experience, that instinctive urge to outrun the rest of the herd, and to summon all of us to watch it.

1974 was welcomed by the Comet Kohoutek, which last appeared some 150,000 years ago, a bit before your time, and was expected to pass by again in another 75,000 years, by which time you might be too tired to care. But, as it was, Kohoutek was said to be an event of such major proportions, it would light up the daytime sky like the sun with a 10,000 mile tail trailing behind it.

In that many of us were of a particularly cosmic consciousness at the time, it was a very appealing way to start the new year. In fact, much of 1973 was consumed with speculations and preparations for the grand event. There was a young woman of Scandinavian descent, named Greta, Gerta, Hilda, something like that, who did fantastic embroidery, and who made you and everyone else you knew lavishly embroidered shirts with the comet blazing across the sky. The sheer anticipation, like so much else those days, was intoxicating.

When New Year's Day, 1974 finally arrived, we were able to barely discern with the naked eye a blip on the screen of the vast Colorado sky that seemed to be in the shape of a spheroid and a tail wending its way in the far, far distance. In astronomical terms, its outgassing was said to have been far less than expected. Major party failure, it was. More than a decade later, the band R.E.M. would sing about it in Fables of the Reconstruction (and like Kohoutek you were gone). By the time Bob Dylan and the Band came to town for a February show at the Coliseum, you were more than ready for something dependably cosmic. That wheel was on fire, rolling down the road. If your memory serves you well.

That year was one of note for the Duck Lake Commune, too, through no fault of its own. This idyllic spot above Ward and the Peak to Peak Highway, just off Brainard Lake Road, was for many years the retreat of an amorphous group of women who valued their privacy and largely kept to themselves.

Unfortunately, rumors were rife in the mid-seventies that they might be harboring one of America's most wanted and notorious fugitives. The heiress, Patty Hearst, was on the lam. She had been kidnapped, beaten, and raped, she later claimed, by the Symbionese Liberation Army, an extreme example of academe gone berserk and a particularly violent fringe group with very rabid political orientation, not to say: pretensions. Whatever the truth of that very bizarre episode in the tales of the culture wars, and Hearst's participation in various bank robberies, bombings, and the rest of that gang's oeuvre, a time came when most of the SLA was dead or in jail and Patty Hearst was nowhere to be found.

Your gallery on Broadway was up the street from the Carnival Café, which actually occupied the original site of your place plus the place next door that once housed the Little Kitchen, Boulder's first vegetarian eatery. This café was run by Mark Gunther, who created something like food as performance art, or maybe craft, anyhow. If Ringling Bros. opened a delicatessen that featured not pastrami but brown rice, maybe this was its spawn. Acrobats served your salad, jugglers handled and handled and handled your drinks, and eventually, you got to eat.

And once when you were eating there, a very nice couple confided in you that yeah, Joni Mitchell, and yeah, Stephen Stills, and yeah, those old Beat poets ate there, but dig it! The other day, right over at that table, that one right there – and here they leaned in close and very confidentially told you – that's where Patty Hearst had lunch! Now, that's celebrity!

Seems they knew for a fact that all those Lezzies up at Duck Lake were hiding her out, helping her recover from this police state assault on her person, and doing what was right by her – but you have to keep it quiet, dig? So many people came to tell that story that you had to wonder how it was the Man hadn't heard it and long since taken her down.

The story gained enough traction that reporters were sighted more than once at the Commune, peering through windows and knocking on doors. Later, too, the FBI was said to have come calling. Those very private women who lived there kept their cool, apparently, and later on, when Hearst finally turned herself in and the very convoluted aftermath of her story unfolded, when jurisprudence and society's demands for retribution were enacted, not a word was said about her reputed days at Duck Lake.

Like much of everything else you're discussing here about that time, there was a lot of traffic back and forth from Colorado to San Francisco for reasons of the residents' own, and it was none of your business. But perhaps that was the source of the rumors that became a very rural version of an urban legend. It is said, too, that a cousin of one of your dearest friends was a dead ringer for Ms. Hearst, unfortunately for her. Perhaps that's why the sightings were so regularly reported. Perhaps you'll never know. Like so much else those days, it was a very big story, one so strange that it defied reason at a time you were naïve enough to believe there really was a reason for these things.

One celebrity who was for a time in residence at Duck Lake was Kate Millet, author of Sexual Politics, and one of the women who shook up the status quo in those tumultuous times. She was there with her partner, the photographer, Cynthia Adams, both of them like everyone else enjoying the peace, the beauty, the isolation, and the shared vision of a place where people could be who they were without reservation. They were said to sit down for martinis precisely at 4:00 p.m. each and every afternoon, sipping those cool beverages where they were seated in old metal chairs out front of their cabin, high, high, high in the Rockies.

You may have noticed by now that this narrative has a distinctly male orientation, which is because that's the way it was back then, and for a long, long time beforehand. It was clearly and without much thought given to it a patriarchal society we inhabited, even in the way you all resisted the rest of the established order. Some people were thinking about it, though, most of them female, and they were more than willing to say so. The counterculture had a lot to counter, including long-held, deeply inculcated assumptions about gender roles.

Women had a lot to call attention to, an entire system and a long history to think their way through, and solutions to propose. People like Millet, Germaine Greer, Betty Friedan, Gloria Steinem, Billie Jean King, and lots of others of note started saying so, talking about it loud and clear. Like many of your friends, what they said kind of took you by surprise. It wasn't that you didn't care. It was just another aspect of your life you needed to come to terms with. You had barely slowed down enough to notice. Once you took the time to listen, there was much to be learned, lessons still reverberating to this day.

Fortunately, the shows kept coming. Music didn't heal all, but it was a wonderful salve. Deep Purple, Eric Clapton, a great show by the Allman Brothers at Mile High, and four days later, same place, Crosby, Stills, Nash & Young; lesser acts like Edgar Winter, Black Oak Arkansas, Seals & Croft; and in a stunning show at the Fieldhouse in Boulder, the truly extraordinary Joni Mitchell, who put on a great performance, even though she was distracted by a shutter clicking off photographs through the curtain behind the stage, and she made no secret that she was pissed. She never discovered who it was and you're sure not telling anybody at this late date, Dan Fong. Just sayin'...

1974 came to a rousing conclusion with a boxing match between big, bad, fearsome George Foreman, the heavyweight champion of the world, and former champ Muhammad Ali, who had lost his title to the draft board for refusing to serve (I ain't got nuthin' against them Viet Cong. They never called me "nigger.")

Nearly 4 years later, when the courts restored his right to his livelihood, Ali lost a close decision to Joe Frazier. Smokin' Joe met George Foreman in the ring shortly thereafter and was knocked down 6 times in two rounds before the fight was stopped.

So, Ali and Foreman were finally scheduled to meet in the Rumble in the Jungle of Kinshasa, Zaire, which country had underwritten a large chunk of the guaranteed purse. The fight was preceded by a great music festival with James Brown, the Crusaders, B.B. King, Miriam Makeba, and the Spinners, among many bands that played. Kinshasa was happening. The entire world was tuning in. Everyone seemed to think Foreman was unbeatable and was favoring him over Ali by 7-1, even more shortly before the fight.

But, in your mind, there was only one Champ and it was a once in a lifetime opportunity to back Ali with odds like those working for you. You got $1000 down on him at 10-1 and watched on closed circuit TV for round after round as Howard Cosell told you Ali was being pummeled, "taking a terrible beating," big, bad George continued to flail away, and Ali played his cagey game.

Although he took some ferocious shots, Ali was looking pretty unruffled. Foreman, on the other hand, was looking puffier each round. His face was looking battered and his legs were getting wobbly. When Round 8 was nearly over, Big George was flat on his back, struggling to stand, staggered by a flurry of punches that took him out. He later said, "When I finally hit him my best shot, flush on the chin, he leaned in and said, "That all you got, George?' That's when I knew this wasn't what I thought it was." Ali was Champ again and you were up $10 grand, the best bet you ever made. Later that night you caught Freddie-Henchi at the Shapes and the joint was rocking.

28

OUT FRONT

WHAT ATTRACTED BARRY FEY TO FORT COLLINS again nobody knows for certain. He did the Stones there in '69, and a Savoy Brown-Fleetwood Mac show a couple of years later. Maybe the CSU folks gave him a great deal, although he told you they split the take, which was on the unimaginably generous side of Barry's usual deals.

For whatever reason, he did two big shows there at Hughes Stadium in 1975. It was a pretty good facility if you didn't mind the drive from Denver and Boulder, which had a couple of pretty sizable stadiums themselves. Maybe he just wanted to prove once again that the fans will show up if the music is good. These two shows were very good indeed.

On July the 6th, Chicago and the Beach Boys were double billed and they absolutely killed it. Chicago at that time was at the pinnacle of its long and very successful run. People may not realize this band sold more than 100 million records and charted albums one after another throughout the Seventies. They were huge and they were good, a unique band heavy with horns and great arrangements.

They were produced by Jimmy Guercio, who now owned Caribou Studio in Nederland, and was at the show with a guest named Elton John, who played a few tunes with Chicago. Jimmy had deep ties to both bands. It was no surprise to see him there, with the latest guest artist from the Studio in tow.

The Beach Boys, as Fey was fond of saying, are the only American band who can do a 90 minute concert of nothing but their Top 10 hits. They ripped through their set and, even absent Brian Wilson, were a marvel of energy, harmony, and great tunes. There is something timeless about good music. Theirs was of that era when California was a teenager's dream, hot cars, surf boards, and blondes in bikinis were what you wanted, and the Beach Boys were the window to that world. Ten years later, the dream was different but the memory still resonated and that perpetual youth in you still hoped that Rhonda would help you get her out of your heart. Help, help me, Rhonda.

Two weeks later to the day, the Rolling Stones were back in Fort Collins and they were smoking. By now, there was no question in anyone's mind that this band was the personification of big time rock & roll. This was major league, even in this cow town. People turned out in droves. They gathered hours, even the days before, which upset some of the townspeople who apparently didn't care the University was making a pile of money on the show. Fans were coming from far and wide. This after all was the Rolling Stones. You'd best be ready when they hit town.

They opened with Honky Tonk Women, with Elton John in a cowboy hat on piano, sharing vocals with Mick, and for more than two hours they never let up, although they spent much of it trying to get Elton off the stage. He came and went aimlessly, visible pissing off Keith Richards for being in the way, and eventually drawing boos from the audience. When Billy Preston came on stage midshow for his two songs and moved Elton out of the way of the keyboards, a resounding cheer rolled up from the crowd. Mick later said they didn't give him the boot forcefully "'cause we're all Englishmen."

Other that that, the band was awesome. Ronnie Wood on lead was new, having replaced Mick Taylor, which is no small feat. Even though you knew of him from his time with Rod Stewart and (Small) Faces, you were curious to see what he'd bring to the table. The answer was more than enough. By now the band had so much great material to choose from, they couldn't miss. Ronnie and Keith, Bill Wyman and Charlie Watts played together like what you expected of the World's Greatest Rock Band. Mick as always was Mick. Version three of the Rolling Stones ramped up another level.

This was the era of increasingly elaborate staging, and the Stones were no exception. Many of the shows on the tour were performed in a lotus flower, and most all of them featured a stadium-sized inflatable penis. What it added to the music was next to nothing, as far as you could tell, but that's entertainment. At these prices, which had reached double digits, inflation was a theme.

Stones in the Rockies

From '69 to '72 to '75, the evolution of this band and the business they drove was startling. In just 9 weeks, the Tour of the Americas that year did 46 shows in 27 cities and grossed beaucoup bucks. The 40,000 fans who joined you at the show in Fort Collins made one of the more intimate gatherings on the tour.

"Don't trust anybody over 30!" That was the mantra, the agreed upon way of dealing with the generation gap. They were of another time, another way of being, of thinking. You were young and different. This was your thing, not theirs.

Then one fine May day in 1975, you were 30. You wandered into your gallery sometime around 11:00 that morning. Before you knew it, Otis Taylor, Nick the Greek (whose birthday it was, too, but not yet the BIG one), they and some other folks dragged you off to Potter's for a celebratory lunch.

Yow! Before you'd even ordered a sandwich big drinks began to arrive. One after another that friends sent to the table. Even Otis, who as far as you know never touched liquor in his life, ordered you up a very large tumbler of Courvoisier. For lunch. It was a good time, a lot of laughs, some really great folks, and by the time you staggered back to Oraivi, it was around 2:00 in the afternoon and you were bombed.

There was a dinner scheduled for 7:00 that evening at La Chaumière, where any number of friends were expected, and at this very moment you were pretty uncertain whether you could make it to the couch, let alone to that estimable dining establishment a dozen miles west of Lyons. If ever a superhero needed to appear on the scene, this was it. And she did.

While you slumped against the wall of the gallery, clumsy behind the counter and somewhat blinded by the glare of the brilliant day taking place outside those big plate glass windows, the incredible Leslie breezed through the door. "Happy birthday," she said, and gave you a kiss. "Wow, you look like hell," she added. "Come with me."

It is unfashionable to speak of such things at the time this story is being told but of the time you're speaking about the simple truth was this: Leslie was a babe. Drop dead gorgeous, effortlessly vivacious, and every single heterosexual male in Boulder was hot for her. So when she said, "Come with me," you did.

She led you to the little office where there was some privacy, and with her likewise unfashionable fake fingernails that were a few inches long, she scooped from her bag a generous helping of flake cocaine and tightened you up very effectively. More than once, and more than twice. "Feeling better?" she asked, and, um, yes, you were. Leslie saved the day.

You sailed through the rest of the afternoon, made it home for a shower and shave, and with your partner headed off to dinner. It was a great one, fine food, fine wine, a few bottles of champagne, and a very large table ringed with your friends. Who could ask for anything more?

Well, you didn't ask, but Thom supplied it, tossing you a bindle of what looked like a rock of very good coke. Before deerings became common and grinding up a gram took seconds, there was a ritual that attended the consuming of cocaine. With a single edge razor blade, you sliced and sliced and sliced some more shavings from a rock of coke, and then commenced to chopping and chopping and chopping those shavings into a very fine pile of granules that finally was drawn into thick long lines that sparkled with an ungodly attraction.

So it was with you. After a very long, skillfully executed effort to prepare half the rock for your friends, a large serving plate was covered with a single line that snaked from the rim to the innermost part of the concentric circles. Just as you were about to pass it around the table, the waiter arrived, and this being Boulder in the mid-seventies it was only gracious to offer him a toot. You did and he snorted the entire plate of coke.

There was a rather stunned silence that attended the table as the waiter rushed off to mangle the rest of the night. Once you regained your composure, you calmly prepared and passed around the rest of the rock, which made for a taste for one and all. But nobody who was there that evening ever forgot that moment, and you were given a rather vivid view of what lay ahead in the years to come. The worst part of it all was the weeks or more thereafter the waiter hung around your gallery. You couldn't get rid of him for the longest time.

In 1976, Barry Fey initiated the Summer of Stars concerts at Red Rocks Amphitheater. It was one of his most successful ventures, bringing bands to town year after year for performances in that pristine venue. The story has been told. No need to repeat it here. It was the apogee of rock & roll in Colorado.

Think about just a few of the people who played there over just the next few years: Stephen Stills, Joni Mitchell, Jackson Browne, The Eagles, Willie Nelson, Carole King, James Taylor, Bruce Springsteen, and the Dead maybe 50 times. That so much music was to be had was no longer any surprise. What was different is that it no longer was the voice of a lifestyle. Too many of us were moving on, driven by different motives. The music had moved on, too. But the setting then and forever was ethereal.

What was consistent in the experience you had there was the notion of residual magic about the place. The natural beauty, perfect acoustics, a view from the seats to nearly the curve of the Earth on the eastern horizon.

So many times there the full moon would rise and the audience would murmur, stir, even applaud, and the band with its back to what you were seeing and a very large backdrop of sandstone to hide it could only wonder what was up until that huge orb rose to where they finally could see it, and the music they played lifted with it; you were in a cosmic place where the sounds reached another level of perfection and the heavens seemed to play a consistent role, like that time so many years later when from out of nowhere the lightning flashed across the pitch black sky again and again while Bob Dylan sang "Knocking On Heaven's Door," and Tom Petty looked skyward from the stage, nodding as if to say, "Yep, that's it, exactly!"

The nation's Bicentennial celebration in 1976 was a bit of a bust, it seems. There was no end to the noise leading up to it, coins and commemorative plates, trains traveling from one state to another with all our country's proud heritage of 200 years contained in a boxcar or two of authentic replicas, and a pretty good fireworks show on the 4th of July. Lots of committees working on lots of stuff that came and went like the comet. It's hard to remember anything of consequence about it all. Except of course that Colorado, being the Centennial State, had a half as long an anniversary to celebrate, too. Presumably then it tried even harder than some of the other states that gained statehood less synchronistically.

Fortunately, the concert season had some hallmarks. Elvis himself played McNichols Arena in April that year. He'd played the Coliseum in April of '73, but you were out of town. Clark Secrest said in The Denver Post the show was great, the full Las Vegas monte, even in that ugly facility. This show might have been great, too, but you don't know. You didn't go. Can't say exactly why, but the King no longer moved you, great as he had been, good as he still was. There was too much baggage attached to him now, a story told elsewhere in this book. It was not much more than a year until he'd be found dead, one of the great performers of your time finally silenced. Maybe if you'd known what was coming, you'd have gone. Maybe not. Don't matter now.

When Bob Dylan brought his Rolling Thunder Review to Hughes Field in Fort Collins on the 23rd of May, he was a few days short of 35 years old and, for a notorious control freak, his entourage seemed curiously undisciplined. It was deemed a band of gypsies and the stage was littered with them. In some cases, it was hard to tell who was playing what instrument, if any.

The show was hampered, too, by a steady rain that turned the grass field into a mud bath by the time 25,000 people had walked, run, danced, slid on their bellies, and otherwise traversed it. You walked the edge of the stands, which were relatively dry, spent some time trying to identify the performers for a piece you had to write, and otherwise just tried to dig the music and the fans while a soft rain continued on and off to fall. You spotted Mick Ronson, T-Bone Burnett, and the violinist Scarlet Rivera, no slouches there, but the energy seemed to be less than what you expected.

The music itself was fascinating, the beginning of what became for Dylan a persistent, ongoing reimagining of his songs. Familiar as they are to everybody, with every new tour and each new band he gave you brand new interpretations.

He and Joan Baez sang many a duet on songs they'd sung together in the day when he was struggling to make a name for himself and she, as reigning queen of folk music, was his gateway to the big time. "A see through blouse and nobody wants to," he said of her in Don't Look Back. But he was so much older then. He's younger than that now.

This day, they gave new interpretations to "Hard Rain" and "Blowin' In the Wind" and he was in especially fine voice while she as always was a pure, clean, and clear soprano. There were times when the music seemed a bit scattered, and the band somehow as often as not sounded tired. There's no other word for it. When you learned later the show had been recorded for what became the Hard Rain album, you had a chance to revisit it. It wasn't anywhere near his best. Dylan is always worth hearing and so it was once again, but less so this time around than many other times you had the pleasure.

What none of us knew at the time was that this was the last rock concert ever at that friendly football stadium. Neighbors sued to stop the shows because the "noise" annoyed them. That and the riffraff that came to hear it. Dylan one day would become a Nobel Laureate for the noise he made but it mattered not. It might fly in Stockholm but not in Fort Collins, not at Hughes Stadium ever again.

If nothing else came of the Centennial, it ushered in the first important season in the history of the Denver Broncos, who for the 17 seasons since their founding in 1960 had been doormats of pro football. When they finally won the American Conference championship in 1977, riding on the strength of its famed Orange Crush defense, which limited the opposition to an average 17 points per game, things were finally looking up. They beat the hated Oakland Raiders in the championship game, and when all-star linebacker Tom Jackson near the end ran to the Raiders bench and shouted at opposing coach John Madden, "It's all over, Fat Man," the tide finally turned.

Madden was a pretty good coach, and later a noted broadcaster of the "common man" school but he gained great wealth and fame from becoming a brand for an early and still successful video game. Like Michael Jordan and Nike in the shoe stores, Paul Newman and salad dressing in the grocery stores, free enterprise finds a way to put your name to use. Nothing comes between me and my Calvins. When that "me" in those jeans is Brooke Shields, you notice.

There were a lot of good concerts at Mile High over the years, but only a few good Broncos teams. Like music in Colorado, their fan base was huge and loyal. At last, their patience was to be rewarded. For the next 40 years, the team's winning percentage would be among pro football's best.

Their first Super Bowl appearance (and second, third, and fourth, for that matter), however, was less successful. You and your friends had convinced each other that the 11 points the Dallas Cowboys were favored by was a joke. The Broncos gave up very few points. Hold Dallas to 17, score one touchdown, and they'll have covered the spread. You all agreed to put some serious money on the Broncs. Yes, you did.

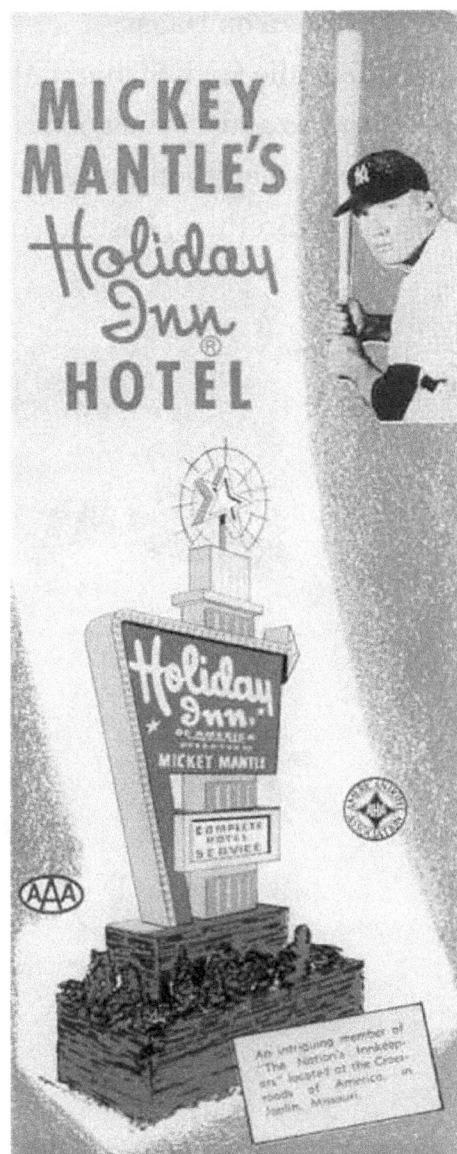

MICKEY MANTLE'S *Holiday Inn* HOTEL

You were traveling in a remote part of the country, holed up in the Yogi Berra suite at Mickey Mantle's Holiday Inn in Joplin, Missouri the day of the big game. The night before, in a bar in Kansas, you met a Texan who explained to you in no uncertain terms that the Cowboys were going to destroy Denver. "Do yourself a favor, son," he told you. "Save your money. I bet my entire ranch and all my cattle on this game, and I don't doubt for a minute how it's going to turn out." He was pretty convincing.

After the game, which Dallas won 27-10, you and your friends connected by phone. "Wasn't it awful?" they said to you, and you agreed it was. "I lost a thousand bucks," one said. Another said, "$500." "How much did you lose?" they wanted to know. "Uh," you said, "you're breaking up on me, can't hear you very well" and hung up the phone. You just couldn't find a way to admit, at the very last minute, that the guy in the bar hooked you up with his bookie and you got a bet down on Dallas.

Unlike Mile High Stadium, there were some pretty good football teams at Folsom Field in the Seventies and a lot of good concerts, too: Fleetwood Mac, The Eagles and the Steve Miller Band, and a marathon concert that harkened back to the festival days when, in May of 1979, The Doobie Brothers, Boston, Poco, Bob Welch, and Country Joe McDonald took the stage.

©Dan Fong 2018

The Doobies were huge in the Seventies, progressing through several different iterations, each with its own sound and different personnel. For much of the latter two-thirds of that decade, after Michael McDonald and Patrick Simmons held sway, they were pretty tightly connected to Boulder. Marty Wolff and Dan Fong were very involved in the band's tours, and Michael Barberi and Bobby Lakind were on the road crew. Lakind, one of the guys on the construction crew that remodeled your gallery in Boulder in '73, eventually joined the band on both drums and backup vocals.

Maybe the best of all the Folsom Field shows was the Rolling Stones in July of 1978. Folsom Field holds about 60,000 for football. There were nearly 75,000 to see the band, which was at the height of its powers now, and these stadium shows were old hat for them. They had it down. There weren't any screwups in the shows anymore. The sound was perfect, the stage was perfect, the sets were razor sharp. Backstage was maximum security. Your pass only got you so far. Then there was another set of hurdles to clear. Only the band, Barry Fey, maybe Tony Funches and L.C Clayton, and very, very few others got past that barricade.

This show was a more stripped down, back to basics version of the band. The crowd loved it. There was a point late in the concert, as one great tune followed another, "Honky Tonk Women," "Just My Imagination," "Beast of Burden," "Miss You," a couple from Exile, "Happy" and "Tumbling Dice," and a couple of Chuck Berry tunes, they played "Brown Sugar" and "Jumpin' Jack Flash" back to back, and when you looked out over that vast sea of people on a perfect summer afternoon, there were waves of energy visibly moving from the stage through the entire crowd and back, lifting and settling whole rows and sections of people like one complete, connected organism roiling with pleasure and fully attuned.

That moment of complete synchronicity between band and fans, where the music makes them one and they're joined on a common wavelength, is an extraordinary moment when the power of the art we make, and the instinctive way we respond to it, simply transcends all differences and the things that come between us. Maybe those differences align harmonically so that we make music rather than noise. We meet on some higher level of consciousness as one people. Something is completed in us, made whole for the moment, and it's phenomenal for the time that it lasts.

As lofty, pretentious, and granola-soaked as that can sound when you have the nerve to state it out loud, it seems to you to be the essence of what everybody in this way of being has been trying to accomplish, not as a moment but as a lifestyle, naïve as the aspiration may be, unobtainable as the goal. There are unique places and rare times when those sensations are experienced. You may spend much of your time on this Earth trying to find your way back to them.

But there are the other times, too, when reality reasserts itself in your life and clobbers you with a fist in your face. It seemed in the mid-seventies that ideology was a fulcrum you sat astride on one side and opposite you was one or another personification of all the ways of living you wanted to resist. Despite your best efforts and an abundance of reasons to keep trying, there was no simple means to effect the change you hoped to see. The traditional ways had so much power behind them. There is said to be a deep and abiding truth in every cliché. This seesaw seemed to be balanced between spirit and instinct. Dreams perhaps were giving way to doubt.

29

UNDERCOVER

THERE ARE MANY VERY STRANGE STORIEs you could tell about these times. Some of them require you to be very careful in the telling, and this is one of them.

At the height of the culture wars, when the tide began to turn against the widespread insurrection that was the youthquake, the media had conscripted the movement, drugs and debauchery had worn it down, and the spirituality had given way to craven bouts with cocaine in every corner, nook and cranny of the day, Elvis Presley came to town.

This was not the Elvis of chapter one, the brilliant kid reeking of talent and a new kind of energy that lit up the stage. This was older Elvis, post-hep cat, post-army, post-movies, post-Vegas, post-toasted with pharmaceuticals of every kind.

This, too, was Elvis the cop-groupie, who got tight with the narcs at DPD and was visiting them on a regular basis. It was widely, if deferentially, reported that the King showered his entourage of cops with expensive gifts and eventually purchased them a fleet of Cadillac and Lincoln Continental convertibles.

Think about that! One, two, three, four, can we have a little more…? Just what does it take to earn the King's beneficence?

Ron Pietrafeso, the bull goose loony narc of Denver, who often took the stand in court cases prosecuting kids for drugs and swore that he could tell a drug user just by looking in his eyes, this very same officer of the law was for a time the lapdog of the King, reportedly taking him on drug raids that were timed specifically so that Elvis could fly into town and participate.

You were told on more that one occasion by more than one person in a position to know that a photograph exists of Elvis in a Denver Police Department uniform with a gun in his hand at a narcotics raid. Much as you wanted to see it for yourself, you never laid eyes on it and have no proof of the veracity. It makes for a wonderful if particularly chilling story that may be nothing more than urban legend of a twisted kind. Maybe not.

But you remember the night in the mid-Seventies, when cocaine had taken hold to an irresistible degree, and the paranoia and self-absorption that attended it had polluted nearly every gathering of the times; and, there were a half-dozen or so of your acquaintances sitting around drinking beer, smoking herb and snorting a few lines, then a few more.

A fellow you didn't know had joined you and one of your friends said, "Oh, man, I hear you got busted" and he said, "Yeah, what a drag." And the talk went into the why's and wherefore's, the who's and the what's.

At a point well into the conversation, which ebbed and flowed with the drugs and the various levels of enthusiasm for hearing about it, he finally said, "What's really weird! You're gonna think I'm crazy. I can hardly believe it myself.

"But, I swear to god, when the bust went down, all these narcs with guns came busting through the doors, screaming at the top of their lungs and the guns shaking in their hands, they were so amped. And here's the really weird thing: the guy who drew down on me, shoved a .38 right in my face and sneered at me, the dude looked exactly like Elvis Presley. Swear to god, he did."

When Elvis expired on a toilet seat in his home at Graceland in 1977, the autopsy revealed he had more than 10 different drugs in his system including levels of codeine at 10 times the prescription level. Although he had been in good health for most of his 42 years, the last few years of his life were grotesque. After his death, his personal physician was revealed to have prescribed more than 19,000 pills, tablets, vials and injectables to Elvis in the previous three years. More than 17 whacks a day.

It is an especially ugly ending to a storied career, but with all the other things it brings to mind, you can't help but wonder about handing a man in that condition a gun and inviting him to join you in a high pressure venture like a narcotics raid. You also can't help but wonder what Pietrafeso saw when he looked in the eyes of the King.

This is another such story. Ron had more than one myopic moment in his notorious career as a narc. He moonlighted for a few years as the personal bodyguard of Michael Balfe Howard, scion of the Scripps-Howard media empire and recently arrived in Denver as the editor and publisher of the Rocky Mountain News, one of their flagship papers which was locked in a ferocious circulation battle with The Denver Post.

Howard began his reign in Denver as a muckraker, going after cops on the make, graft and corruption, malfeasance at City Hall, a dependable strategy for making a name and goosing the circulation. He caused quite a stir and people began to take notice. Before he knew it, though, he somehow had acquired some high rolling cops as his personal entourage and Denver's numero uno narc as his bodyguard. He also had acquired a helluva coke habit.

When it began, no one knows. Pietrafeso says he never noticed it, even after Howard reportedly drew a very large pistol on a patron at Trader Vic's in the Cosmopolitan Hotel downtown, threatening him in a very loud voice with severe bodily harm in front of a roomful of witnesses. It was becoming glaringly apparent that Howard had a problem. His behavior became increasingly erratic. But his bodyguard said he didn't notice. Not the flaming eyeballs. Not the runny nose. Not the shakes. Not the paranoia. Not a thing. Just guarding his person, he was. What's to notice?

Paul Simon sang something about "a man hears what he wants to hear and disregards the rest." That may be the mantra for a man in Pietrafeso's position. What you hear and what you see is what serves your purpose. If you are his bodyguard and he signs your checks? Well, you probably don't look too close. If he is too distracted to carry on his campaign against the Department, well maybe that's all right, too. Howard was visibly flaming out in front of all the city and his personal bodyguard never noticed his charge had a serious habit. Perhaps, once again, he never looked in his eyes.

There are dreams and there are nightmares. Dreams of a fall from grace. Dark flights through realms of loss. Places you don't want to be. But, there you are. Friendless, it seems, because the people with you in this place are mocking you, moving against you, turning away from you. This is the future, you see.

You dreamt one night about your friend who peddled dope. You went to his house to score an 8-ball. He raised his eyebrows and shook his head, saying, "Well, okay" with resignation, mocking your habit, the one he feeds. He went to wherever he kept his stash. Steppenwolf was playing. You looked around and saw that everything you ever owned, and everything your friends ever owned, was hanging on his walls, covering his floors, filling his display cases, furnishing his rooms. Like a bank, it was. Or the Repo Man. "Goddamn!" the music said.

Another night, another dream. This one longer, more involved. Scary, too. Charismatic coke dealer, living large, very righteous, so he says, very hip, got the blam, got the clothes, the cars, the girls. The difference, he tells you, between the men and the boys is the size of their toys. Maybe there are other differences, too, you think to say, but he isn't listening. Spirituality was last week's news. He's on to other things.

Many years of this go by. He's cruising. Living in overdrive. Getting larger, more full of himself, puffed up, kinda bloated even. 'Til the shit comes down. His patron gets busted. They've got it on tape. Both of them. Phones tapped. Cameras in the ceiling. Dead to rights. Many transactions over the past many months. Dude looks different, seen from above. Like he's wobbling.

He comes around. Asks for your help. Needs cash for lawyers. Has some people who want to make a buy. Big buy. He knows you know people. Can you hook them up? No, you say, you don't do that. What do you mean? Just make the introduction, he says. All you gotta do. For a friend.

There's a soundtrack, too. "Miles Smiles." "Thriller." "We'll Be Together Again." It plays when he's there and it plays when he's gone. When he's back with a very good-looking young woman, the music has changed. Champagne and party, she's all about fun. All up tempo. Go, cat, go. Whatever you want. Gonna party like it's 1999. Brings her around your place. Brings her to parties with mutual friends. Please come by my place later, she says. She has to show you something. A lot to show, she has, when she greets you at the door. You run the other way.

These are his people, he tries to tell you. They want to meet yours. You tell him no. You don't have people. Just your friends. What the hell is this all about? He won't let up until you tell him to get lost. He finally goes away.

A thought you simply can't accept keeps coming to mind. He's trying to set you up. He's trying to SET YOU UP! She's obviously a narc. You know it. How can he not know it? You simply can't believe it. Nobody would do that to a brother. Would they?

Well, guess what? He turns state's evidence against his patron. Guy who floated his boat all those years. Testifies in open court. Sends him up the river for maybe 20 years. Mr. Cool does 90 days. Hard time, no doubt. Disappeared from the scene after that. Only for a while. He's back online making noise again. Hardly a dent in his smug demeanor. One who knows, you know? That's him. The man who invented Boulder. Hear him tell it. Just another once upon a time brother, jive talking again.

Nobody should have dreams like this. These are people from the very beginning. You've known them forever, looked up to them, believed in them. But once the cracks appear, caverns of doubt open up in the construct of your life. Why do you have these dreams? Maybe you really don't know those folks at all. Maybe, too, you really don't yet know yourself. But you're getting to know the future.

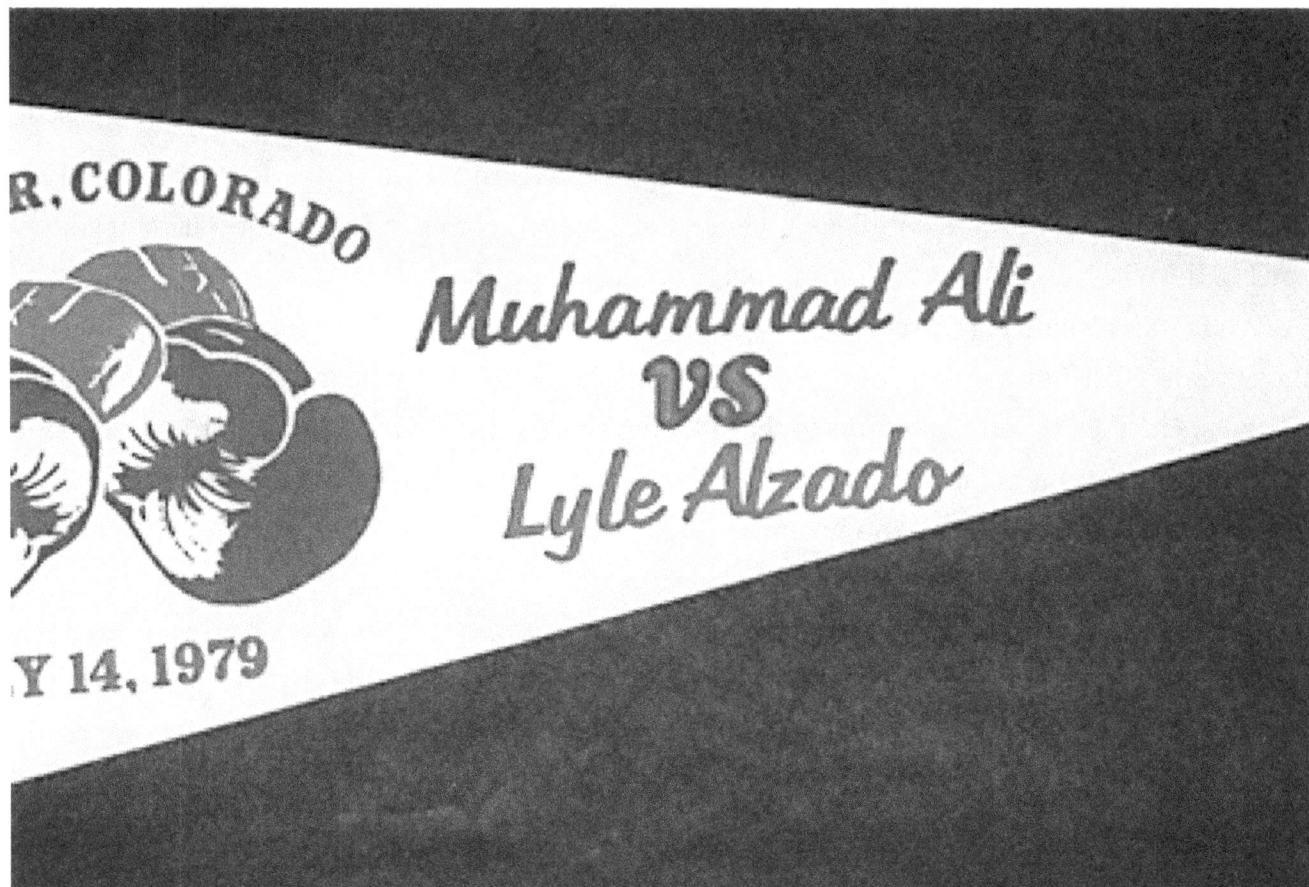

R, COLORADO
Muhammad Ali
VS
Lyle Alzado
Y 14, 1979

30

CHAMP

YOU MET A LOT OF PEOPLE who were becoming famous, and all of you were really just kids, so it never seemed like that big a deal. You only got tongue-tied once, and that was when you met The Champ.

When you were young, the champ was Sonny Liston, heavyweight boxing champion of the world. He lived at the other end of the block from where your folks lived. He was big, bad, and surly, an ex-convict with a very unsavory past and an entourage that ranged from known thugs to a much greater champ in his own time, Joe Louis, whose spouse served as Liston's attorney.

If you worked up the nerve to knock on the door and ask for an autograph, the door would quietly close in your face for a minute or two. Then one or another very large man would hand you a tiny piece of paper torn from a tablet on which was written, "Sonny Liston." It obviously had been composed in advance, hard to say by whom. Sonny didn't write fast or willingly, if at all.

He had come to Denver from Pennsylvania for reasons that were unclear. People said it was to get away from the police in Philly, where he was notorious before he was champ. It wasn't long before the Denver Police Department got to know him, too, but meanwhile, people in the neighborhood tended to keep their distance, sightings were rare, and every once in a while the garage door would open and a big black Cadillac emerge, presumably with Liston inside.

For the most part, the LA section of Park Hill was a quiet neighborhood in those days, so it was a very big deal when all hell broke loose one sunny day in May of 1963. In the exact center of the front lawn where it fronted Monaco Parkway at 35th Avenue, immediately in front of the sprawling ranchstyle home of red and blond brick, there was parked a tour bus the size of a Greyhound and written on its side in large, bold letters was: Cassius Clay – I Am the Greatest!

Kids gathered from all over the neighborhood to stare at the sight and only after a moment realized there was a young man standing between the bus and the house, waving his arms, jumping up and down, screaming at the top of his lungs: "Come out here, you big, ugly bear. I'll whup your ass right here. Right now. You so ugly, yo' mama in hidin'. 'Shamed to show her face. I am the greatest! You chump! I want you now! You no champ. You a chump. I'll whup up on you so bad, you know who is the man. You know who is the champ. I. Am. The. Greatest!"

You and everybody else looked at each other and wondered: who is this guy? No sign of Sonny Liston, not even a flutter behind the curtains on the big picture window out front. After he ranted and raved, jumped up and down, did some very fancy foot work and threw a few dozen punches, Clay and a bunch of other young men climbed back on the bus and drove away, leaving very deep divots in Sonny Liston's lawn.

There would come a time not all that much later when you would travel to the opposite side of the world and live for a few days in a very remote camp on the Afghani border with Russia, and, in a place where no one spoke anything like English and they honored their guests with a pitcher of milk from a goat spiced with its blood from a neat incision in its jugular vein made right before your eyes and butterfly-stitched neatly back together; where finally there was neatly back together; where finally there was a place in which not a single soul had heard of Richard Nixon, the American president soon to be disgraced, but where with gleaming eyes and big, wide smiles, nodding very vigorously, yes! Yes! Muhammad Ali? Yes! They would confirm that there, too, like everywhere else, they knew of the most famous man in the world.

And, so, when you and your friend, Thom, went looking for the Champ on a fine June day in 1979, when he was in town for the weigh in and all the other antics of promoting this "match" next month, it was with the deepest admiration and respect that you sought him out. Muhammad Ali was a seminal figure in the zeitgeist of that turbulent and promising period of our lives. He was the Champ in every sense of the word, a towering and emblematic figure who stood for exactly the sort of pride, defiance, and independence the rest of us in our own small way hoped to emulate. Ali was courage writ very, very large.

To stand by yourself in a corner of a ring in front of the entire world, where in the corner opposite you Sonny Liston, Floyd Patterson, Big Cat Williams, Jerry Quarry, Joe Frazier, George Foreman, Ken Norton, Ron Lyle, or Leon Spinks are there with only one intention and that is to beat you into submission, to face that time and again puts your courage to a test most of us can barely imagine. A few of them beat him. Once each. He beat them in rematches, sometimes more than once. No one was bigger, braver, more courageous than Muhammad Ali.

But, too, he was at the end of his career. Having just regained the world heavyweight championship for the third time, and widely considered to be by far the greatest heavyweight fighter of all time, despite being deprived of four of the prime years of his career for having refused to be inducted into the U.S. Army (I ain't got no argument with them Viet Cong, he said, when the biggest, baddest opponent of them all, the USG, was in the opposite corner), Ali was 37 years old and officially retired.

As something of a lark, and for what reasons no one is certain, he agreed to fight Denver Broncos All-Pro defensive end Lyle Alzado, he of the Orange Crush and Denver's first if failed Super Bowl appearance, who was maneuvering for a new contract and threatening to turn his underpaid skills back to boxing, where he once had enjoyed a respectable career as a Golden Gloves fighter. It was an 8 round exhibition to take place at Mile High Stadium on July 14, 1979 and, as it turned out, nobody was particularly interested in seeing it, much to Alzado's regret. He mortgaged his house to finance the match and it bombed.

But you wanted to see the Champ and so you and Thom cruised around the various venues in Denver where a celebrity like him might stay and, lo and behold, as you made a left off I-25 onto Hampden Avenue and took a long look at the parking lot of the Marriot, you couldn't help but notice a fleet of long black limos parked near the entrance. Kismet! You are there.

The lobby gave way to a number of broad hallways heading in various directions. You stood there, taking a long look down one and then another, not knowing what to do or how to begin. Just then, a commotion ensued and from far down the cavernous reach of one hall an entourage emerged.

There were many dozens of very large and sharply dressed men, a few very fine looking women, and a variety of mismatched characters moving in concert together. In the center of the crowd, an aura of light like a renaissance painting about him, was Muhammad Ali. The Champ himself. In the flesh.

You and Thom stood there and the crowd moved toward you, insiders all of them apparently, and you were not. When the Champ came near, you stepped toward him and for just a moment, the only time in your life when celebrity got the better of you and you felt tonguetied to be in his presence, you stammered and stuttered, cleared you throat and finally were able to say, "I wanted to ask you about your foundation," and Ali himself stopped walking, looked at you, sized you up, took you gently by the arm, led you to a bench and talked to you alone for 5 or 10 minutes or more about what he wanted to accomplish for world peace and righteousness with the foundation he had just established. It was mesmerizing to be the subject of his attention, and when he finished what he had to say, you shyly asked if he would mind an autograph for your daughters, which he gave you, shook your hand, and disappeared back into the maelstrom of being Ali.

All these big events were taking place, and you were in the middle of it, maybe too busy to notice things were changing, that the sound track had a lot of static suddenly, the pace of your days and nights seemed to be carrying you along. When was the last time you found a moment to gather with your friends in a group, ask about each other, listen to what you're told, be in no hurry to move on to whatever else was clamoring for your attention? When was the last time now was more important than next?

You think about these things that were taking place and how far it was from the founding spirit of this counterculture movement that you cherished. Where was the wonder that brought you together, the belief in each other that so profoundly made a community of a bunch of kids on the move? What happened to that desire you all had to make something different of the world you found, to reach some place higher? What the fuck, already?

How did it all fall apart so quickly? How did an entire part of the population so quickly become untrue to itself? We became me became I. That seems to say it all. But it doesn't say why.

Maybe it is because all of you stood in the way of irresistible forces. You were on the wrong side of the counterculture equation. Culture as a bacterium that grows relentlessly, each cell replicating itself in cycles that eventually rise up and cover anything in its way with a thick blanket of ravenous organisms that feed on you from the outside in, until you too are one with the organism and you join it in devouring the next host, and the next. Counter that, right?

Ominous signs gathered. You tried not to notice. Things were changing in your little town, and in the world at large. Beware the rat fuckers of Southern Cal. As if Mr. Richard Nixon didn't warn you. Perhaps it is unfair that you associate those changes with the Boulder Partnership and its commercialization of Boulder, with that god awful, made by non-natives, motherfucking mall.

But, in your mind, on your clearest, cleanest, most agreeable, least prejudiced day, that abomination of an urban initiative was the little liquid turd dropped by a bird on a slope in the snow that rolled into a ball and gathered momentum as it headed downhill, gaining in sheer size and mass and velocity until it reached the exact center of Boulder at Broadway and Pearl, where it erupted into a patently hideous image of somebody's dream of a real estate catalyst that turned the entire innocent, unsuspecting town, that wonderful, welcoming, gathering place hard by the Flatirons at the foot of the mountains, as pristine, unsullied, and unpretentious a place to live, love, work, and wonder as any you could ever hope to find, to arbitrarily turn it into a vast shopping mall of unbounded pleasure and posturing, where the very wealthy could put their trust funds to good use buying the real estate and building the mansions from which they could venture forth when the moment moved them to sumptuously dine and shop and otherwise expend their monies grandiosely for maximum effect. What's the point of having it, after all, if you can't lord it over those who don't. And if not here, where better? Sic transit gloria, fair city that you loved.

The terrible truth, all these years later, is that everybody, EVERYBODY, loves it. Boulder is a gem in the ocean of ostentatious living, the bon mot of what it is to be and be seen in this glorious country of ours. Wear it well, folks, and enjoy! Lost times are not found again.

You disappeared back into the maelstrom of being you. It was a lot to do, just keeping up with that.

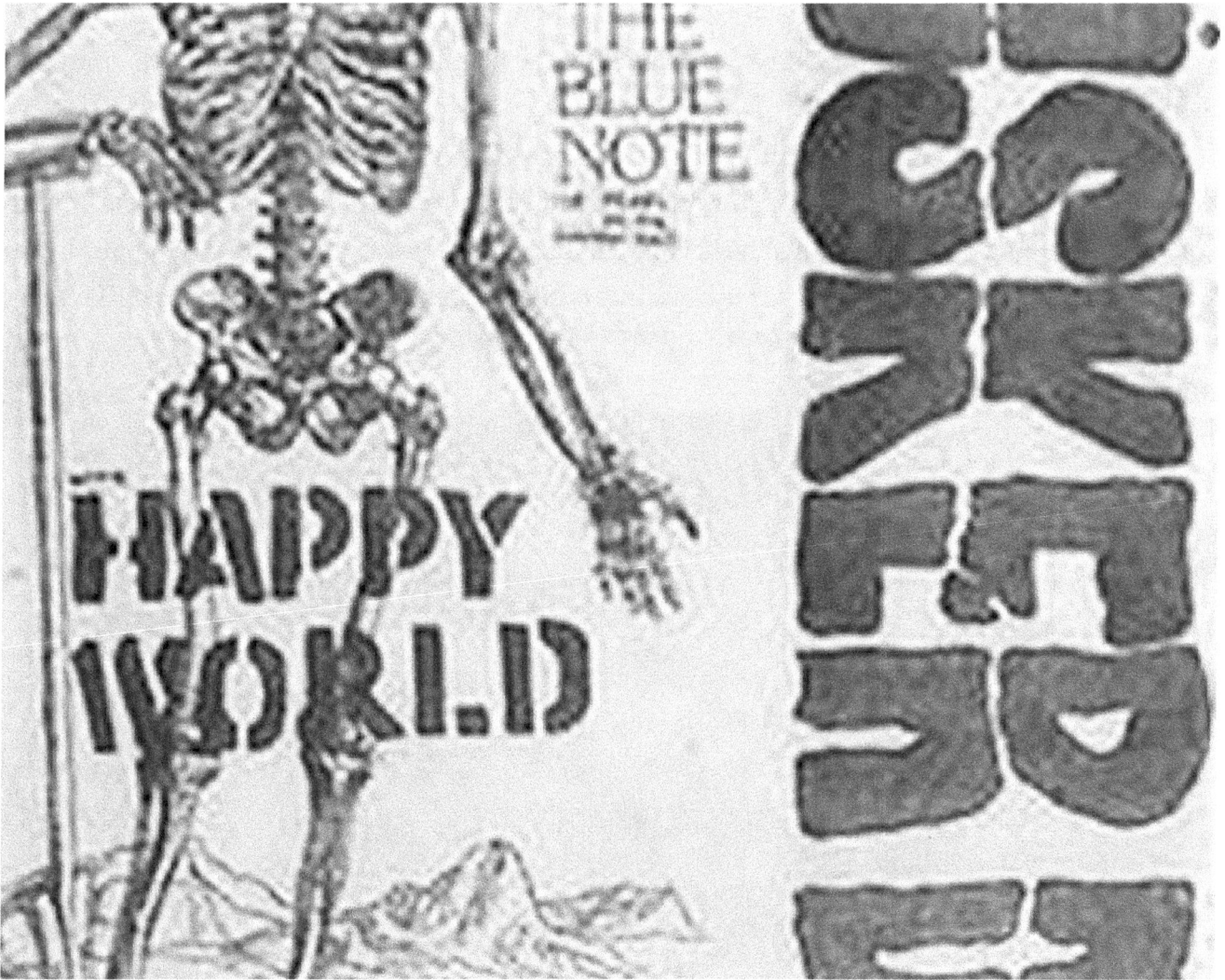

31

END NOTES

A CLUB FOR THE TIMES APPEARED ON THE MALL. The Blue Note. Jenny Grantham's place. Sweet place it was. Great bands to be heard. You saw any number of them at the end of the Seventies. Most of the time, you were hammered. So was everyone else.

Dizzy Gillespie, who played his crooked, soaring trumpet for an amazing set one night. When he came back from the break, he stopped in front of the ravishing Linda Wearley and simply stared at her, wide-eyed, smiling, nodding a little, pure admiration and more than a little hustle. You were too fucked up to care, but you noticed. Finally, he took the stand and played only the congas while his very hot band ripped through Night in Tunisia and Salt Peanuts, all the stuff they do. Dizzy was waxed by the altitude, blew himself out the first set. Still, a wonderful show.

Van Morrison played an incredible show there, his huge voice booming through the room, doing a lot of songs from Moondance, in your mind one of the very best albums of the time. Morrison was not a great performer when he began, but his gigs got better and better. What he always was, though, was one of the two or three best singers ever to come to us from the United Kingdom, an Irish tenor with power and range that is breathtaking to hear. When many years later you heard him sing "Before the World Was Made," one great Celt paying homage to another, it was a moment that made you glad you'd lived long enough to share it. Up the Irish!

Who else? You remember Rick Danko. Not The Band but pretty good. With Paul Butterfield, no less. The Ramones. Wynton Marsalis. Maybe the Go-Gos, or did you just dream that? Some of the local players. A lot of big names no longer recalled.

VAN MORRISON
HIGH IN COLORADO
BLUENOTE 90
BOULDER, COLORADO
NOVEMBER 22, 1978

What you remember best is the sounds of the breathing, the wheeze, the rattle, the shake, the sheen. Cocaine was oozing out of every pore. Of everybody in the house. One night at the end of one gig or another, the band long forgotten, the club was closing, the audience exiting, and no one particularly was looking forward to going home just yet, at the door in this town famed for extraordinarily beautiful women were two absolutely stunning chicks. They sized up the players as they filed out the door and to those who looked promising said quietly but very clearly, "I'd do anything for some coke. Anything." The inimitable JR looked at his pals, Martin and Douglas, raised his eyebrows and widened his eyes, and simply pointed at the two women. From that moment onward, they were a foursome for many months to come.

If there is an elevator pitch for this story, it's that young people who were unwilling to accept what they were offered had the courage to try something new. It wasn't easy, it wasn't encouraged, but the time was right and numbers were on their side. The constraints they broke free from unleashed a time of unprecedented creativity. It was apparent in lots of different endeavors, but especially in the arts. And the art that was most directly attuned to the moment was music.

Music was a powerful voice for the times. It was a rallying cry, but also a gathering place. It was something that was yours. A focusing device, if you will, a constant reminder that your job on this earth is to have fun, to be joyous, to love your brothers and sisters, to be charitable, to be kind. All the good stuff. It was an Eastern perspective applied to a Western way of being.

Ain't nothing wrong with making a buck. We all gotta do it. What we want to think about is what we are and aren't willing to do to make it. That's really what it was all about. What do you stand for? Where do you draw the line?

Musicians face those choices, ask themselves those questions. They lived in the spotlight and we got to watch. Artists from time immemorial have dealt with those ethical and aesthetic questions. When does art let commerce in its pants, and just how far does it get to go? By the Seventies, though, it was lived out up close and personal. The crowd was watching.

And, in truth, there is reason to suppose that the excesses of rock & roll stardom provoked the urge to collapse the edges of integrity. You are getting back to the earth, living in a shack in the woods, maybe running water and just enough electricity to drive the turntable, and Mick is riding in a limo from one gig to the next, staying in a suite at the Carlyle when he's in town. God bless him. He did it his way. So, the question is, what is your way?

Hmm. Maybe you should move a few ounces of blow for your friend, just to raise enough cash to overhaul the tractor. Maybe a new refrigerator would be nice. Keep those organic cutlets nice and cool. What did Karen Kismet say: The way to satori is to renounce your desires? Uh, did he say announce my desires? Well, I want...

By now, you're back in Denver, living in a home in the servant quarters part of the Country Club neighborhood. Ellie is teaching grade school, Deva is a Brownie, you are contending with the snow storm. The music is muted these days. It all sounds like your heart beating in your ear.

When you look around the neighborhood where you live, there are all these young people in very good clothes with labels prominently displayed on them, driving very nice cars with large logos affixed to the grills, and shopping in very fine stores where they hand you your merchandise in very fancy bags. They carry themselves as if it all matters. Very. Much. So.

These are Yuppies. Young Urban Professionals. Back to the city with a vengeance. Back to the life. People who want to make it. Who have the hunger. For nice stuff. Good neighborhoods. Big jobs. Power lunches. Status. Things that show and tell. They are bought in. Big time. Asking no questions. Except, how much? Got it or not? That's all they want to know. About themselves. About you.

You wondered where they came from, who the fuck they were, what it was that provoked them? Your once for a while brother-in-law said that you—that first wave of all the baby boomers—got all the good stuff. He and his contemporaries got what was left. Mostly merchandise and posing. Maybe that was it.

Your introduction to the Choices was LSD. Theirs was cocaine. It took a long while before the blow laid waste to everything that you and all your friends held dear. Those deconstructed visions of truth and consequences. Blown away in a snow white wind. You got to ride a lot of ponies before the devil mare.

That's where they started. On the back of the Bitch. Saddle up. Kiss your ass goodbye. There is no you, there is only me. Sadly, you get it. You've been there. You know all too well where it lives.

A lot of good came from those times. The world was not remade, but maybe it tilted a little on its axis. The prevailing winds returned after a while and the big engine of commerce commenced to hum again. The dominant ways were reinstituted, but maybe they were not quite the same.

Much of what you and all your friends believed in found a place in the parade. All these years later, you remember those times and what they came to mean. Now you have perspective to apply whereas then you had only hope.

There are tenets of what many of us believe today, the ways of doing what we do, that carry the DNA of the counterculture. While society at large more egregiously than ever worships at the temple of commercialism and bows down in awe of wealth, no matter how it's earned,

there are places here and there in our communities and our culture that harken back to a vision more naïve perhaps, but maybe more courageous, as well.

Clean air, clean water, whole foods, locavore, biodiversity, stewardship, the Big Blue Marble, human rights, civil rights, equality, equity, diversity, inclusivity, and, ironically, for that cadre of believers, a very healthy dose of skepticism, about power — government, corporate, and individual power, and how it is applied. Question authority! Always. Don't follow leaders. Watch your parking meters.

Like youth itself, there was that remarkable moment of freedom you struggled toward as a child growing up, wideeyed with amazement and nearly hyperventilating sometimes with the excitement of it all. You wanted to be cool about it, but it was all too much!

It was like seeing something dazzling just outside the window of your little room, and when you finally ventured through the door into the world out there, sometimes the sun is shining, or the rain is falling, lightning is flashing across the sky; or maybe a blizzard commences, the wind howls; or, in the midst of a frozen Colorado evening, a chinook rolls down the mountain front from who knows where to warm you. It's a comfort of a sort you've never known before and you're just astonished that you get to be part of it.

To remember this time in the history of Colorado, a time not so long ago, really, and yet the landscape is barely recognizable, as if it all was fiction. That has been the challenge. The future came hurtling at us like a bullet train, a mere pinprick of a point on the far horizon that before we knew it arrived full bore and blew up in our face. Welcome to the here and now. What turned out to be merely a brief moment in time, though, was magic, pure and simple.

Music was happening all over the country, and many cities were visited by these bands as part of the magical mystery tour. But in Denver and in Boulder, these shows were happening night after night. There was a specific gravity created that drew more and greater numbers of people to it. It weighed on us. And lifted us!

It was truly an abundance of riches, so much so fast that your only regret is not to have seen and heard even more of it. When you're in that lane and the traffic just keeps coming at you, you assume it always will. When it's gone, and sooner or later it is, you wish you had been even more present than you were.

The soundtrack of your life was a rich one, full of incredible music that came your way, day after day. The musicians, the club owners, the radio station personnel, so many people in so many different ways took a flyer on a new way of doing things, a last gasp of independence before the business was brought back into the holding pen and all those wild creatures tamed or put to sleep.

Freedom, brief as it was, allowed a cornucopia of creativity to pour forth, a passionate vitality of artful, joyful, spiritual living that was unlike anything any of us had seen before. It was completely unprecedented and no one knew what to make of it nor how it would turn out. But enough of us were willing to take a chance and see for ourselves where it took us. And we did.

In the center of it all was this dialogue between all of us and the music, which heard us and spoke to us. It was a way of living with a soundtrack of brilliant music and fabulous entertainment. It had a soul, too. Don't ever forget it.

It's very unfashionable to praise promoters, those gross, money-grubbing, heartless business people who actually made you pay for the shows. Artists are inclined to believe in their heart of hearts that they should gather crowds of worshipful fans merely by picking up a guitar or a paintbrush, and beaucoup bucks then will descend on them like spring showers. Put your memory to work and your fingers to the keyboard and maybe your story will sell itself. Maybe not.

Somebody had to deliver all those goods, bring them to town, book the theaters, promote the shows, sell the tickets, fill the stands, pull back the curtain, and let the music rip. For that, you're thankful, too.

That part of your life was made possible by Hal Neustaedter, Harry Tuft, Barry Fey, and Chuck Morris. There were many others, too, who played a role, but those four people brought big time music, live and in person, into the little towns where you lived. It wasn't New York, nor L.A., but Colorado reaped an incredible harvest of music at a time when the music mattered, and it was because of the vision, the talent, and the timing of those four men.

Among them, they brought nearly every musician of merit in the music business to town, everybody you ever wanted to hear, a lot of people you didn't know enough to know you wanted to hear, and people who became not just the soundtrack but even the fabric of your life.

As always, of course, it is the artists who produce the magic. It is art in all its forms that makes life profound, calls to us, gives us clarity, shows us a way, points to those totemic moments we encountered and reminds us of what we are in danger of forgetting. What it was! But someone has to do the work to bring them to us and us to them.

What all of you were together in that place and time, promoter, producer, manager, musician, painter, scribe, announcer, artist of every sort, and audience, what all of you had in common was something that always made you wonder.

Harry Tuft, sage gentleman that he is, summed it up for you at the end of an interview you and Dan Fong did with him early in this century, now that he and Fong and you were older and all these things were warmly, if sometimes only dimly, remembered. You mused about all the many and various people who made up these memories and the different ways they had of making the story what it was.

It was a tribe of individuals living in a fascinating period of history, where everything was changing and nothing much seemed certain. Nearly every kind of character imaginable had crossed paths with you, it appeared, some you loved, some you liked, some you cared for less than others when all was said and done. Something brought you all together in that amazing and unsettled time. "The one thing we had in common," Harry said, "is that we all loved the music."

— END —

CREDITS

A note about credits in the age of the world wise web: everyone wants and deserves credit for their work. Not everyone gets it. In the age of the Internet, photographs of virtually anything you want to illustrate are available, usually in many different places, and most often without naming the photographer.

Wherever the photographers of the pictures included in this book could be identified, permission to use their work was sought and they are named. Where a picture was found on several different sites with no photographer named, the site we copied the picture from is credited.

We extend our sincere thanks and appreciation to the photographers and designers, known or not, who have illustrated this work. Like all those of us who make the effort, what we produce has a chance at immortality. We hope this book will be another small boost to keeping your work alive.

Front Cover: Dan Fong (danfongphotographer@q.com)

iii   Ibid

1   courtesy the author

2   medium.com

3   Carolyn Cassady, 1952, courtesy nealcassadyestate.com

4   Westword

5   Black American West Museum/National Register of Historic Places

6   colfaxavenue.org

8   Colorado Heritage Extras

9   Denver Folklore Center

11   unknown per Dan Woog (06880danwoog.com)

12   wikipedia.com

13   wrongsideoftheart.com

14   BuffaloNews

16   2.bp.blogspot.com

17   ipinimg.com

18   colfaxavenue.org

19   unknown

21   tO.gstatic.com

22   unknown

23   udiscovermusic.com

24   allmusic.com

26   courtesy Craig Swank: kimsloans@wordpress.com

27   Rocky-52.net (above)

27   Carnegie Library for Local History (below)

28   Ibid (above)

28   unknown (below)

CREDITS continued

29   triumphmotorcycles.typepad.com.

30   Columbia Records

32   cpr.org

33   People.com

34   bestclassicbands.com

35   youtube.com

37   onedrawingdaily.com

38   Capitol Records

39   dissentmagazine.org

41   The DenverPost.com

43   dailydot.com

44   Baum, Dan: Truth, Lies and Audiotape. 2012

45   unknown

46   unknown

48   courtesy Craig Swank (kimsloans@wordpress.com) (above)

48   allmusic.com (below)

50   Dan Fong (danfongphotographer@q.com)

51   Carnegie Library for Local History/Boulder Daily Camera

52   ABC Probe

53   dailycamera.com

54   Carnegie Library for Local History

56   Dan Fong (danfongphotographer@q.com)

57   Discogs

58   Stephen Collector (www.scollector.com)

59   Boulder Chamber of Commerce

60   Aaron Spong: fineartsamerica.com

61   everon.50megs.com

63   DianneStromberg.com

64   courtesy Clark Richert: Drop City Archive (above)

64   Ibid (below)

66   courtesy David A. Casey

66   Ibid

69   courtesy Lucretia Weems

71   Dan Fong (danfongphotographer@q.com)

74   Ibid

CREDITS *continued*

75   courtesy Family Dog Productions

77   KFML.org

81   Dan Fong (danfongphotographer@q.com)

82   rockinsights.com

83   EncyclopediaofAlabama.org

85   courtesy David Givens: Zephyr-Official.com

86   theguardian.com

87   republicofyoublog.com

88   Dan Fong (danfongphotographer@q.com)

91   TheDenverPost.com

92   passthepaisley.com

93   courtesy the author

94   Carnegie Library for Local History

95   Ibid (above)

95   Ibid (below)

96   TheDenverPost.com

99   Ibid

101   vividseats.com

102   KFML.org

103   courtesy the author

104   Dan Fong (danfongphotographer@q.com)

105   martinguitar.com

106   Stephen Collector (www.scollector.com)

107   unknown

108   Carnegie Library for Local History

109   George Wharton James

110   courtesy the author

112   Ibid

114   lange.com (above)

114   AlbionMonitor.com (below)

116   abovetopsecret.com

117   Carnegie Library for Local History

118   Ibid

119   Dan Fong (danfongphotographer@q.com)

121   unknown

www.ingramcontent.com/pod-product-compliance
Lightning Source LLC
Chambersburg PA
CBHW080530090426
42733CB00015B/2535